Denis O'Connor trained as a psychologist and teacher. Throughout his career he taught in schools and lectured in colleges and universities. He holds a doctorate in education and psychology and has contributed widely to academic books and journals. He is retired and presently lives with his wife Catherine, and two male Maine Coon cats, Luis and Max, in a remote country cottage in Northumberland.

D0237680

PAW TRACKS
AT
OWL COTTAGE

Denis O'Connor
Illustrations by
Richard Morris

Constable · London

Constable & Robinson Ltd
3 The Lanchesters
162 Fulham Palace Road
London W6 9ER
www.constablerobinson.com

First published in the UK by Constable,
an imprint of Constable & Robinson Ltd, 2010

A copy of the British Library Cataloguing in Publication Data
is available from the British Library.

ISBN: 978-1-84901-640-7

Printed and bound in the EU

3 5 7 9 10 8 6 4 2

I wish to dedicate this book to the memory of my uncle, Captain John Watson of the Church Army, whose library of the classics was a reader's treasure chest for me.

This book is also for Catherine, my wife, without whose loving support it would not have been written.

CONTENTS

BEGINNINGS

My extraordinary life with Toby Jug, the hybrid Maine Coon cat whose companionship and love gave me such happiness during my twenties and thirties, sadly came to an end in 1978 when he tragically died. We had enjoyed life together since I had rescued him as a tiny, sick kitten lying alongside his dying mother and brother. Owl Cottage, with its beautiful garden and rural setting, became our refuge and sanctuary over the eventful years we shared together. After his death the poignant memories of him were too sorrowful for me to carry on living there.

In 1980 I moved to Newcastle where I already had been appointed to a lectureship at the University of Newcastle upon Tyne. Later I worked at Durham University tutoring students in Educational Studies until I retired in 2000. In 1998 Catherine and I were married and since we were both contemplating early retirement we began to look for properties in rural areas because of our attachment to North Northumberland. Fate took us in hand and I was able once more, with Catherine at my side, to return to Owl Cottage and revisit the home where in my younger life I had spent such happy and memorable years with the cat called Toby Jug, whose adventures inspired *Paw Tracks in the Moonlight*.

Returning to live in Owl Cottage at West Thirston was for me the consummation of many years of longing to escape the city for life once more in the countryside. West Thirston is one of a group of hamlets, extending eastwards to the town of Amble and the North Sea, which lie astride a rocky ridge above the River Coquet. Owl Cottage is built on a site adjoining a minor road which leads westwards to Linden Hall, Rothbury and beyond. No doubt the area occupied by the cottage has witnessed many habitations throughout the ages but the present structure is built almost entirely of stone and dates from around the middle of the nineteenth century. The front of the cottage runs parallel to the road, leaving the back, which faces south, secluded and private.

The garden is extensive and comprises over fifty trees of various kinds including oak, beech, whitebeam and birch. There is also a small orchard of apple, pear, plum and nut trees, and a meandering swathe of grass bordered by flowering shrubs and flower beds, giving an overall effect of a woodland glade. Wildlife is welcome here and thrives in the pesticide-free environment. My wife Catherine and I refer to the garden as our 'Shangri-La' because of its beauteous tranquillity and natural appeal. There are stories from local folk who say that it is enchanted and inhabited by fairies, although we cannot confirm this from our own experience. Yet on summer nights, whilst songbirds are singing their songs and slanting sunbeams create green-grassed areas of golden meadow, there is an enraptured feeling about the garden at Owl Cottage.

It is certainly a wonderful place for cats and has been much loved by them, not least by our four Maine Coon cats respectively named, according to age, Pablo, Carlos, Luis and Max. These special and affectionate cats comprise our family and their unique and fascinating personalities and activities form the basis of this true to life account of our lives together with them at Owl Cottage. In many respects this book is the continuation of the story that began in *Paw Tracks in the Moonlight* because returning to the cottage and describing the adventures of our present cat family have revived the memory of some additional tales of the legendary hero of Owl Cottage. After all, Toby Jug's spirit endures in every tree and stone there.

PABLO

Pablo was the first kitten to live in Owl Cottage since the death of Toby Jug and we welcomed him, quite literally, with open arms. He was a pedigree Maine Coon. In appearance he was surprisingly large for such a young kitten, with a pointed face and extra large ears. His front paws were enormous and he had a long fluffy tail. His eyes were golden brown and his coat a cinnamon colour like oak leaves in autumn, with some darker markings which would become more distinctive and elaborate as he matured. Pablo had the build and markings of his ancestor, the Norwegian Forest cat.

On his birth cum pedigree certificate he was formally named Pablo Picatsso, son of Billyboyblue and Huffenpuff, and was officially designated a brown tabby. He was born in October 1999 and given to me as a present by Catherine, my wife, who had lived at Owl Cottage with me since we had bought it in 1998. Pablo proved to be a wonderful cat, affectionate and lovable, and he provided us with many fascinating insights into cat behaviour. But perhaps first I should relate how it happened that we acquired Pablo in the first place and how I and Catherine came to be living once more at Owl Cottage. Despite my earlier protestations – at the time deeply felt and firmly held

– at long last I had returned to the home where Toby Jug and I had been so happy in the past.

It all began in the spring of 1997 when Catherine and I decided to take a holiday in the north of Crete. One beautiful sun-filled morning, as we sat on the veranda of our apartment looking out over the azure blue Mediterranean, we heard a cat calling. It was not a distress call, just the kind of cat-talk that some felines make when they see something interesting or wish to express their feelings. I looked over the grey rocks and scrub that extended away from the holiday chalets. In the distance was the mountain known locally as Zorba's Rock, which reputedly was the location for the famous Greek dance sequence performed by Anthony Quinn in *Zorba the Greek*.

Suddenly, I spotted a small figure scurrying straight towards us. In a moment a neat and very petite charcoal-grey, short-haired she-cat introduced herself to us. She was obviously accustomed to people, since she immediately commenced purring and brushed herself against us in the most affectionate manner. I realized at once that she was focused on an agenda which was meant to manipulate us. No doubt she was in the habit of exploiting the charity of kind-hearted holiday-makers. This greeting display by the cat undoubtedly served her purpose which was to remind us of our obligations as hosts. And so it was that a late breakfast of corned beef and boiled ham was served up to her and very well received. I admired her social skills and wondered just how many other tourists had fallen under her spell and been cajoled into offering handouts.

My assumptions about her motives were soon confirmed because she came to visit us every day for the rest of our stay and we became quite fond of this dainty little beach cat. Each time we fed her we were, of course, rewarding her friendly behaviour and so, in terms of psychological theory, reinforcing her activities. Likewise she, this clever little cat, was reinforcing my act of feeding her by jumping on my knee and purring her thanks as a reward for me. Cats are great manipulators of humans and our guest cat proved no exception to this rule. She would arrive either mid-morning or teatime and, having been fed, she would linger next to us, sometimes gracing one of our laps as we relaxed and watched the sun go down. For the moment she had adopted us.

I really liked her, but then I always find it hard to resist a friendly cat. Catherine was not so sure. She is concerned about stray cats when we are abroad in case they carry disease. I tend to fuss the cats I meet on our travels and usually they respond well to me, and so I attributed nothing out of the ordinary to our visiting cat and simply enjoyed the contact for what it was worth until something extraordinary happened on the last day of our stay which gave me pause for thought.

Since our flight departure time was at some unearthly hour during the night we spent the early morning packing and then went for one last trip around the north of Crete in our hire car. We drove first to Maleme and the site of the German War Cemetery. We found it to be a peaceful and poignant place covered in an abundance of deep-red wild flowers which outlined the precisely placed granite-grey headstones stretching out of sight in regimented rows. All was kept in perfect order and obviously tended with great care and reverence for those who had given their lives in the Second World War. We then decided we would just about have time to go on to Agios Stefanos for a brief visit before returning to the apartment. We drove south through the countryside to this tiny tenth-century church which is reached by following a narrow track shaded by oak trees. En route Catherine, to her great pleasure, discovered on the bankside a rare white cyclamen for which this place is famous. *Cyclamen creticum* is found nowhere else in the world. The delicate white flower quivered slightly in the gentle breeze from the sea as we walked by. We were even more pleased we had made the decision to visit the church when we saw its thirteenth-century frescos of the Nativity and Pentecost which were still showing clearly after all this time.

Too soon we had to leave for Chania and make our final preparations for home. This last trip, however, had filled us with special memories of Crete to carry home with us and dwell on at our leisure. We were not back in our apartment until late afternoon and therefore I did not expect to see our feline friend again. But, just as evening was settling in, a frantic scratching at the balcony door roused me from a restful doze. I slid back the door and there she was, anxiously greeting me, tail up and mewing her request for a late supper. After feeding her I sat out on the balcony to keep her company. Together we watched the remains of the day, the last of the deep red sunset over the sea.

Soon she showed her gratitude by slipping on to my knee from where she treated me to a resonant purring session. I was at pains to explain to her that I was leaving and would not see her ever again but I would always think of her as a friend. Since I was talking to her in English and the language of her country was Greek I couldn't be sure if she understood me at all, but then I have heard tales of cats having the ability to read minds and I suspect it might be true. As the last glow of the setting sun changed to a darkening pink, she rose and, without a backward glance, disappeared amongst the rocks. I retired inside the apartment to snatch a couple of hours of sleep.

Some few hours later as we prepared to leave I realized that I had left my sunglasses on the balcony. As I opened the glass door and walked on to the balcony I almost trod on something. In the darkness I couldn't at first see what it was. Stooping to retrieve it I was amazed to find myself holding a short length of vine on the end of which was a single, ripe, red tomato. My wife's urgent call for me to hurry up or we'd miss our flight startled me out of a whole range of emotions that suddenly surged through my mind. Covertly I placed the find inside my jacket pocket. Thinking about the incident during our flight home I felt confused and uncertain. What was this about and why had it happened?

On our local walks I had spotted miniature tomato plants in cultivation on the outside walls of some of the houses in the surrounding residential area, but there were none near our holiday apartment. Part of me felt that I had been given a coded message. Had the cat put the tomato there as a goodbye gift? Why a tomato? In the subdued lighting of the aircraft, whilst most of the passengers, including my wife, were sleeping, I carefully retrieved the fruit from my pocket. The little glistening object lay in the palm of my hand, undamaged in any way. It reminded me so much of a tiny red ball. A cat I had known a long time ago had loved to play with red balls and had stolen some tomatoes from a neighbour's greenhouse to supplement his supply. His name, of course, was Toby Jug. I began to conjure up a scenario that this was a message of some kind, the significance of which was about to unfold. Weary with thinking about it I fell asleep with the thought that only time would tell.

One of the most irritating things about returning from holiday is to find the space behind the front door jammed with a bulk of mail, most of it of the junk variety. Searching through the accumulation, a postcard caught my attention. It was from Carol, one of our friends, and it simply said, 'Have you seen that Owl Cottage is up for sale?'

The feeling that raced through me at that moment was electric. Was this a coincidence? Or did it herald tidings of a change in the air? Was this related to the present of a tomato from a cat in Crete? I began to feel that somehow, in a way unclear to me, destiny was nudging me towards a reunion with the past. Such a return was not now out of the question since both Catherine and I were contemplating a move away from Newcastle upon Tyne. With this move in mind, since we both loved the countryside, we had been looking at properties for sale in Northumberland but had not searched the locality where I had previously lived. We discussed the news about my old cottage at length and then decided, on impulse, at least to have a look at the place and agreed to view Owl Cottage as soon as it could be arranged.

Then something else occurred which resonated with everything that was currently happening. One night I dreamed that I was living back at Owl Cottage as it had once been. Everything was extremely vivid and real. I was taking a walk along a path between the River Coquet and a line of oak trees where Toby Jug and I often went during a summer evening. Suddenly, he was there before me looking resplendent and radiant with glossy black-and-white fur and sparkling green eyes. 'There you are!' I exclaimed, almost as if our meeting had been arranged and I was expecting him. He ran to me and greeted me in his familiar fulsome manner by leaping on to my shoulder and rubbing his face and whiskers against my cheeks. After a short while he jumped down and ran a few yards ahead, turned and stopped to face me. Then a voice spoke clearly in my head: 'When can we be together again?' Startled, I realized the question was somehow coming from Toby Jug. Taken aback with surprise I stuttered helplessly to find an answer. 'I don't know.'

Then came the next question: 'Will it be soon?' Feeling the shock of disbelief at what was happening I groped again in my mind for an answer as best I could. 'I don't know when, Toby Jug, but whenever it is it will fill me with joy to be with you again.'

Finally, the voice said, 'I'll be there waiting for you.' And with a flick of his bushy tail he disappeared. I looked around searchingly but he was nowhere to be seen.

When I awoke the dream was fresh in my mind as if it had really happened. The memory of it was so surreal it bothered me all day. I couldn't dismiss the thought that perhaps the dream was somehow related to some of the other things which had recently happened, stirring up reminders of the past. A further consideration was that the dream happened to coincide with the initial launch of my book, *Paw Tracks in the Moonlight*, and overwhelming feelings of nostalgia at considering a return to Owl Cottage.

The estate agent made an appointment for us to view the cottage. As we drove back to the place that was filled with so many memories for me I could not stop wondering how the cottage had fared without me and Toby Jug. When we arrived and I gazed once more at Owl Cottage my heart missed a beat and floods of emotion and an overwhelming feeling of yearning for what had been swept through my mind.

As soon as Catherine and I stepped into the hallway I was saddened to see how neglected the place had become. Everything was in a pitiful state inside and also outside in the garden. But as we looked around my distress was suddenly lifted by a wave of good vibrations which, as we both recollected later, we felt at about the same time. Intuitively, I could feel the cottage crying out for us to take care of it and make it whole again. It was a cry from an old friend and it touched my heart.

That night in a pub in Newcastle upon Tyne we talked it over and I discovered that Catherine felt as I did and we decided to sleep on it before coming to a decision. The next morning after breakfast we were still both of the same mind and determined to go ahead and make an offer which hopefully would secure Owl Cottage for us.

When at last the sale was completed and I had the keys in my hand it was October and the countryside was bathed in vivid autumnal colours. As I turned the corner into the quiet village lane I stopped the car by the thick wooded copse on the side of the road. Ahead lay Owl Cottage, bathed in bright sunlight. My eyes were drawn to the gate pillar at the entrance to the driveway where a pink floribunda rose I had planted in the 1960s still bloomed robustly. Something had brought me back here – call it nostalgia or just a longing to recapture the sentiments of happy times past. I felt my mind whirling with a multitude of images. For a moment I was overcome with blissful remembrances: I was home again at last.

One of my first duties would be to pay homage to the old apple tree where Toby Jug had been buried. I stood near his grave for a long while to tune back into the ambience of the cottage garden and how everything used to be. When I previously lived at Owl Cottage I had often sensed good feelings in the surroundings, in the very walls as well as the garden. Possibly these were emotional resonances of the lives of people who had spent fulfilling times here in the past. Now I simply longed to renew my relationship with the cottage.

When we took possession it was like I had never been away and I rejoiced in my heart at the homecoming. Happily for both Catherine and for me the cottage seemed the right place for us to be, although there was much to do to make it comfortable. My thoughts turned to remembered times with Toby Jug. He was by now a distant memory yet his image was always with me, couched somewhere in the back of my mind. It was because Toby was so very dear to me that the shocking experience of his death led me to have to leave the cottage. At that time I felt that I could no longer bear to live there without him. He had been such an important part of my life. Although kind friends and neighbours had offered me kittens to replace Toby I could never bring myself to accept any of them. In the light of my feelings at that time it wouldn't have been fair to the kitten, however desirable, because I would have constantly compared him to Toby Jug who was, to my mind, irreplaceable.

By the time Catherine and I were more or less settled in, with all the essential repairs and improvements to Owl Cottage having been carried out and the interior painting and decorating finished as well, it was the beginning of July the following year.

Now July is the time when the Felton and Thirston Fair is held and I must confess that going to the fair to witness all that enthusiasm for the egg-and-spoon, three-legged and running-backwards races, amongst other events like crockery-breaking and chucking-the-welly, does nothing for me. I just want to slink away and hide. In this respect I am not at all the socially minded person that, by nature, my wife is. I therefore really did not want to attend the fair at all. Catherine had other ideas. She had entered one of the flower competitions in the spirit of joining in and also because that year she was particularly proud of her roses. She thought her Rosa Remember Me with its bronze, yellowish orange petals, stood a good chance of winning a prize. So despite my protestations I was prevailed upon to go and I am indebted to Catherine for evermore for dragging me there against my will.

As my wife was enjoying herself making the rounds of the local stall-holders, I managed to slip away to a remote corner of the field to examine a vintage bus. With its elongated bonnet and bulbous headlights perched on top of huge wide mudguards which protected the wheels, it was just the type of bus Catherine and I travelled to school in during the 1940s and early 1950s. Fully occupied in having an in-depth discussion with the enthusiast who owned the bus, I failed to notice the figure of my wife tearing across the field towards me with a look of 'I told you so' on her face. She wasted no time in breathlessly telling me that there was an exhibition tent with a range of pedigree cats on show. Then she triumphantly told me that one of the booths was reserved for Maine Coon cats.

With my mind in a whirl of expectation I duly arrived at the tent. It almost defies description to give an account of the exhilaration I felt as I entered and gazed upon the most beautiful cats I had ever seen. In a corner was a bench on which lay a creamy white and red she-cat that looked to have been fashioned by the Walt Disney Studios. She was the first pure-bred Maine Coon cat I had ever seen outside the pages of a book, apart from the severely injured mother cat I had rescued on the night that I found the half-dead kitten who survived to become Toby Jug. I was totally overwhelmed and entranced at the same time.

On meeting the breeders, a couple called Jane and Dave who subsequently became our friends, I immediately placed an order for a male kitten. We agreed that both Owl Cottage and ourselves had waited long enough without a cat with which to share our lives. Perhaps with a new cat in my life here at Owl Cottage I would be able to lay to rest the ghost of Toby Jug. Time has a way of healing sorrows and now I felt it was the right moment to allow another cat into my life. We decided to call our new kitten Pablo because, after an eventful short holiday in Madrid, we were imbued with an affection for things Spanish. I recall the first time we were invited to visit Jane's house and to choose a kitten from the litter of six.

Catherine was somewhat shocked as she preceded me along the hallway of Jane's house to be confronted by the largest domestic cat she had ever seen. His name was Hamish and he was the alpha male Maine Coon of the household. He was most definitely inspecting us in case we posed any threat. With his large head and intelligent eyes I thought he was marvellous. Catherine was rather more uncertain. When we knelt to peer into the cushion-lined box which housed the squirming kittens I could feel Hamish scrutinizing us and as I turned two fierce golden eyes met my gaze as if to warn us that that these kittens were under his protection. By now, much to my amusement, Hamish was circling the box housing the kittens and glaring at me for daring to handle one. 'It's alright, fellow,' I said to him affectionately. 'Your kitten will be safe and much loved by us.'

Over a cup of tea and a pleasant chat we discussed some details with Jane about caring for a pedigree Maine Coon cat. Then Catherine insisted that I do the choosing and so I hand-picked a burly kitten who appeared to be already asserting himself over the rest of the litter by standing in a biscuit tray and making unmistakeable kitten growls to prevent the others from eating until he had his fill. I picked him up and had a good look at him. I was impressed by the firmness of his chunky little body. After paying a deposit to secure the sale we were told to expect him in the regulation three months' time. And that is how we chose Pablo and subsequently took him into our home and into our hearts.

Now that we had chosen a new kitten I felt that the yawning gap in my life, brought about by the demise of my exceptional Toby Jug, had been satisfactorily bridged at last. With it I felt a sense of relief, as if I was making a new start. Once again, whatever I was doing day-by-day would be enhanced by the company of a cat, just as it had been for the greater part of my life. Even as a baby I remember the silky and furry presence of a cat called Fluffy, a kitten given to my parents as a wedding present. The company of cats has always been a source of comfort to me and throughout my childhood they served as playmates and as imaginary confidants who would listen to my problems and, by doing so, help me to sort out what I should do.

I have always talked to my cats and I always believed that they understood me. The Ancient Egyptians apparently ascribed divine powers to their cats in the conviction that they possessed supernatural powers and many people have noted their mysterious air of awareness of things that mere humans cannot perceive. A notable example of this was an article in the *New England Journal of Medicine* in 2005 which reported on a very special ability which a cat living in a care home for the elderly displayed. He could predict when an inmate was about to die and would visit that person and stay with them, presumably trying to comfort them, until they passed. How the cat named Oscar was able to identify in advance with remarkable accuracy the particular patient who was about to die mystified the medical and care staff at the unit.

The doctor in charge of the nursing home, David Dosa, who was not especially fond of cats, came to realize that Oscar, just an ordinary black-and-white tabby, had an almost psychic sensitivity to human beings. Dr Dosa wrote a book called *Making the Rounds with Oscar* about life at the nursing home and about how Oscar the cat helps staff and inmates there.

Most certainly, from my own experience, I have noted how sensitive my pet cats have been to my mood states, especially when I have been upset. On such occasions I have become aware that my cat has attempted to soothe and succour me by a friendly presence on my knee and the balm of a session of vibrant purring. I must admit, despite my lifelong exposure to cats, I remain at a loss to understand fully what a cat is all about.

A cat, Sigmund Freud might have said, is just a cat, but William Shakespeare might well have added: 'What a piece of work is a cat.' Coupling these two statements together highlights the ambiguities with which cats are perceived. To me, they are extra special animals, not least because, by tradition, they have the most prodigious capacity for survival against the odds. Hence the popular saying: 'Cats have nine lives.'

As the tales I tell in this book reveal, even if many cats look alike, they are not the same by any means. Just like people, each individual cat has a unique personality of its own. But this personality is only likely to reveal itself to humans where the relationship is a close one.

For instance, cats who spend most of the day resting and sleeping, and are put out at night, sometimes have only the most superficial contact with the people they live with. In this environment the cat's relationship with the people in the house might be very basic and consist merely of being fed, watered and given a place to sleep during the day. As a result the cats will tend not to show how interesting they can be because they need unconditional love and attention to bring that out. Put simply, it is necessary 'to make something of them' in the same way as one nurtures and encourages the development of a child. Given these conditions a whole new world of cat 'personality' is opened up as the cat feels secure enough to show its real self. The early days with our new Maine Coon cat reveal something of what I mean.

It was a bitterly cold day in March 2000 when the kitten called Pablo arrived at Owl Cottage. No kitten could have had better preparations for his coming than he did. There was a pedestal with a fur-lined tunnel, two platforms and several scratching posts. There was a large cushion-bed for him, a warm blanket, feeding and drinking bowls, and an elaborate enclosed litter box since we were advised not to let him roam freely until he had been neutered at the age of six months. We had been informed that there was a rule affecting pedigree cats involving the necessity for a special licence in order to breed from them.

When Pablo arrived at Owl Cottage we gently placed him on the top platform of the pedestal so that he could have a good look around and familiarize himself with his new home. He slowly looked about, stared hard at Catherine and then focused his huge amber eyes on me. And next, to my astonishment, he leapt up on to my left shoulder, the one always favoured by Toby Jug. I was naturally quite overwhelmed and somewhat nonplussed. I hoped that this would become a habit but regrettably it was not to be. That was the one and only time he jumped on my shoulder in all the nine years he was with us.

The rest of that first day was spent in lots of play activities of the getting-to-know-you kind. True to his cat nature, Pablo immediately set about establishing his own agenda irrespective of any arrangements that we made. This state of affairs became abundantly clear at bedtime. Our idea was that he should spend the night in the heated conservatory where he had a choice of sleeping areas and where his loo-box was conveniently situated.

Since cats are nocturnal creatures by nature we drew back the conservatory blinds so that, if he so wished, he could observe any wildlife going about outside.

On that first night we put Plan A into action. We placed him on a cosy bed-cushion, gave him lots of strokes, left him biscuits and water, bade him a loving goodnight and closed the door. Hardly had we reached the upstairs landing leading to our bedroom than the whining, punctuated by howls, began. Obviously, Pablo had other ideas and was not prepared to fit in with ours. He was clearly indicating that he was not prepared to spend the night alone. Steadfastly, we decided it best to ignore these protestations as we did not wish to encourage our kitten to think that he was boss. However, as cat lovers the world over have come to realize, dogs may have masters but cats make servants of the humans with whom they live. So it was to be with Pablo. The uncertainty about the outcome was soon resolved totally in Pablo's favour.

After an agonizing twenty minutes spent trying to close our ears to the noise coming from the conservatory, we capitulated. When we opened the door we were heartily greeted by a diminutive figure who commenced a welcome dance around our legs and joyously followed us upstairs to confirm his right to sleep where he liked, which in this case was on our bed. After treading his 'I'm getting ready to snuggle down' war dance on our best duvet, he eventually lay above our heads against the headboard with his face resting on Catherine's pillow near, and sometimes on, her long hair. During the night when either of us moved he began a loud husky purring sound which I referred to as the 'Donkey Serenade'.

We allowed him to sleep in our bedroom for a few weeks and then, as he grew accustomed to the house and became confident in our love, he decided that it would be more fun in the conservatory at bedtimes because he had posts to scratch and balls to chase, and sometimes there were exciting things to watch happening outside in the garden at night.

As he grew bigger and matured over the next few months we became aware of his complex and dynamic personality. Pablo's intelligence was remarkable and, short of speaking English, he had his own precise way of communicating with us through cat sounds and body language: he was, as many cat lovers will understand from their experiences, a 'Talking Cat'.

Sometimes when he was in full flow, conversing with us on some priority of his, jumping on our knees and rubbing his huge head against our legs and arms, we would wish he would shut up and give us a rest. But inevitably we would sooner or later realize what it was he wanted. Perhaps, as happened on several occasions, he had upset his water bowl and, fastidious cat as he was, wanted it put right. Or, as happened during his first encounter with springtime outside, there was a cock pheasant in HIS garden and it was bullying him. He wanted us to make it leave. In our life with Pablo we began to appreciate the wide range of sentient responses of which Maine Coon cats are capable, all of which reminded me constantly of how Toby Jug had been with me. Pablo loved our company but was suspicious and often alarmed by strangers. He would respond most enthusiastically to us whenever we focused special attention on him. At other times he liked to lie near us when we were talking together, as if listening to what was being said. I often had the impression that he was studying us as much as we were seeking to understand him. His manifest affection for us was unlimited and we grew to love him more and more as time went by.

There were many impressive characteristics about Pablo which emerged during those early days, often related directly to the special relationship developing between him and me. In late evening, after dinner and before I joined Catherine in the sitting room to read or watch television, I liked to sit alone in the conservatory with all the lights out and stretch my eyes to witness silently what was going on in the garden. I call this my private thinking time. It was winter when Pablo came to us but to my delight he made a habit of joining me, forsaking the warm fireside in the sitting room. He and I would sit together peering into the dark shadows cast by the bare branches of the mature garden trees, many of which I had planted all those years ago. Sometimes the darkness was so absolute that we spotted nothing, but if there was a moon, even if it was merely a sliver, parts of the world outside would open up to us. One night we watched a tawny owl hunting through the trees, a sight which filled me with excitement and sent Pablo into a frenzy, but then he could see in the dark much better than I could.

Since no pesticides or other poisons are used in our garden, it is a haven for wildlife and so Pablo and I shared the enchantment of watching the nocturnal creatures which inhabit the nearby woods and gardens and which often chose to roam about near our trees and bushes to satisfy their needs and wants. Even better, when there is a full moon the garden assumes a fairytale silver mantle in which mysterious shapes move and are revealed as hedgehogs, rabbits and field mice going about their natural ways. They moved in a hushed, muffled manner, unaware of two rapt witnesses, a trembling young cat and a fascinated man, peering through the conservatory windows at the wildlife show outside. On some special nights our patient observation was rewarded and we were privileged to witness a variety of animals behaving naturally. Once we viewed a large mole emerging from the eruption of his tunnel exit to rummage in search of supper and to get some fresh air. One moonlit night in mid-March we saw a pair of hares boxing under the apple trees before racing off to continue their mating somewhere in the wide expanse of the farmer's fields beyond. Most wondrous of all, we once saw a huge white barn owl dismembering and eating what appeared to be a rabbit on the roof of our garage. Unfortunately, she quickly flew off as she caught a glimpse of Pablo's gyrations as he raced back and forwards on the window sill because the sight of such a large bird had sent him berserk.

Of course, on some nights we saw nothing because the sky clouded over or a neighbour's alert lights forced the creatures of the night to seek the shadows. Nevertheless, such times did not dissuade us from mounting a garden wildlife watch whenever the opportunity presented. Although I felt that it was I who was teaching my cat by sharing my interest in watching the nightlife in our garden, I eventually came to appreciate that cats come already programmed not only to know about nature but also intuitively to understand their place in it. Pablo had much that he could teach me and I had a great deal to learn from him. His natural-born skills were far superior to mine. His eyes could see much better in the darkness and his sense of smell and hearing were even more acute than his sight.

I was soon to be shown practical proof of this when I decided to train Pablo to wear a harness and accompany me on night-time walks beyond the confines of the cottage area, just as I had once done with Toby Jug. But first of all I had to persuade Pablo that wearing a harness would increase the opportunities for walks outside the vicinity of our garden and that this would contribute to his overall enjoyment of life.

This was not easy and the first few attempts were total failures. He simply lay down and refused to move. Then I decided on a plan to deny him an early breakfast. I then carried a pocketful of his favourite biscuits with which I enticed him, one at a time, to keep walking. In no time he got the message and began trotting alongside me with his harness on, as long as he received an occasional much-desired treat. Also, he began to delight in being outside in the fresh air. He was only in our garden but it did give him the chance to sniff around, startle little birds and partially climb some trees. Furthermore these garden trips helped Pablo and me to bond closer together and so it was that a stubborn cat turned into a willing cat for our walks. Eventually, Pablo was able to have his breakfast at the usual time, as soon as we got up, and I didn't need to dispense so many treat cat biscuits. We were now ready to travel beyond the confines of the cottage and to experience again the man and cat affinity that I had so enjoyed all those years ago with Toby Jug.

Since I am by nature a night owl, a habit formed in student days, I am rarely in bed before three in the morning, so I was able to choose to time our first nocturnal excursion as late as possible in order to reduce the possibility of encountering any dogs. We set out at midnight. Above us was a clear sky glittering with stars and a half-moon casting a silvery gleam though the trees. To be out at night in the countryside is an exhilarating experience; it is like being in another world.

We headed along a woodland path, well-defined and much used by anglers. Pablo walked ahead of me, lead taut, sniffing the fresh night air. Soon we heard the sound, of the weir and then saw that the river was in full flow due to recent rains. It was late April and it had rained a lot that spring, which was nothing uncommon in our part of the world. Pablo was buoyant with expectation, turning his head this way and that and raising his nostrils to savour fully the exquisite scents of the riverbank. Maine Coon cats are most highly sensitive to their environment and charged with quick responses to the possibilities of any situation. By the light of the pale moon I could see his body all aquiver with the excitement of exploring and savouring this new environment. I noticed that at almost four months of age Pablo had nearly trebled the size he was when he came to us, but he still had a long way to go in that respect because his breed do not reach full size or maturity until the age of four years.

At last we reached the side of the weir where the roar of the river tended to blanket all other sounds. It presented a picturesque sight as we gradually discerned through the shadowy trunks of the trees the translucent misty vapours rising above the waterfall like ghostly apparitions in the chill night air. Water has a charm of almost universal appeal to people and animals alike. It affects the tired mind like a balm and inspires the soul to contented contemplation. I pushed open the sprung wooden gate that gave access to the path alongside the weir and Pablo pulled me along by his lead in his enthusiasm to explore the way ahead. We stepped out onto the rocks that rose high above the tumbling waters and surveyed the vista before us. Moonlight rendered the gushing streams of white water into cascades of silver spray which splashed against the rock walls above where we stood. We moved along towards a great stony outcrop above the river and I sat down on a huge flat-topped boulder. Soon Pablo, tingling with excitement, jumped up to sit at my side. We shared a midnight feast of pork pie and I drank coffee from a flask. We sat together on the rock in comfortable repose, much as I had done previously with Toby Jug such a long time ago. Time had not visibly changed the river but now I was changed from an eager young man having a fun night-time ramble with his cat to an older, more mature person who was reliving the past in the company of a different cat. This experience was more mellow, but nonetheless memorable for all that.

As we made our way out of the woods I reflected that the trip had proved to be a success for both of us but especially for Pablo, who sniffed obsessively at mysterious animal tracks all the way along our path homeward. As we reached the open road I could see the snowy outline of the Cheviot Hills and in the far distance the Cheviot itself, which brought another raft of memories of a special cat, a horse called Fynn and days spent on lonely trails through the beautiful Northumberland wilderness. That night, before I turned in, Pablo treated me to an affectionate purring session with much rubbing of his body against me. His huge amber eyes conveyed a glowing appreciation for all that he had experienced during our walk. The big cat knew how to say thank you.

In the weeks that followed I took Pablo on many late night jaunts and used the time to train him to respond to my whistle by administering tasty treats. He was a fast learner and I always kept him on a short lead because I knew that there was always the unexpected to consider. How right I was to do so as subsequent events would prove. Our walks together served to give us both a welcome form of exercise since we were each housebound most of the time, Pablo because he wasn't allowed to roam freely yet and me because I was busy writing at my laptop. There was another benefit. The walks that brought us closer together as partners sharing in the raptures and the mysteries of nature also served to tune us in to each other's thoughts and feelings as we went along. But this halcyon state of affairs was not to last much longer and could well have caused the demise of one or both of us.

When Pablo was about five months old and growing larger by the day an incident occurred on one of our walks which could have resulted in serious injury for either one of us or, in the worst scenario, death. It happened during a warm spell of weather in May. We set off from the cottage around half-past-eleven and were soon deep in the woods approaching the weir. As Pablo and I wound our way along a narrow trail, flanked by banks of willow trees on one side and scattered broom on the other, we could hear the thunder of the weir coming closer. Suddenly Pablo stopped and refused to move despite my urgings. I always carried a small torch with me on these night-time excursions and I took it out now and shone it around, thinking that Pablo must have discovered something that I could not see. The torch slipped out of my hand and, just as I bent down to retrieve it, a shotgun blasted twice from very close by and I heard the whistle of the pellets as they ripped through the branches of the trees above and around us. Abruptly Pablo's lead was jerked out of my hand as the terrified cat ran for his life. If I had been standing then I surely would have been hit. Bent double for safety I threw the torch light to one side in an attempt to draw fire away from us.

Hearing men's voices approaching I raced crazily back along the path, tripped twice over tree roots and fell headlong on the rough ground. Eventually, bruised and bleeding from cuts to my hands, I made it out of the woods and stopped panting with the exertion of unaccustomed running. I strained my ears over the thumping of my heart to hear if I was being pursued.

Of Pablo there was no sign. I whistled and called softly and whistled and called again and again, but there was no response. Since it was now after midnight it was really dark, too dark even by the dim light of the stars to look for where a shocked and frightened cat might be hiding. Having regained my breath, if not my composure, I headed for home in an angry and bitter state of mind. What madman would be out at night in an English wood, blasting off a shotgun so wildly? I determined to investigate the matter thoroughly with the help of the authorities but for now I desperately needed to find and comfort my cat.

Soon I reached the garden drive and, as I fumbled in my pocket for keys, a dark form moved out of the shadows and meowed. It was Pablo, unhurt, safe and sound and still trailing his lead behind him. I cradled him in my arms and the stress drained out of both of us. I murmured words of relief with my mouth pressed against the thick fur of his neck and he made little whimpers of what I understood to be sheer joy. We were alive and well, and secure on our own home territory.

The next morning I gave Catherine a modified account of what had happened and she told me off for acting so rashly, confining her sympathy to Pablo who slept, as cats do when troubled, the entire day through. Later I telephoned the police and explained what had happened. The response was unsympathetic to say the least and amounted to a verbal reprimand for my alleged stupidity in wandering the woods at midnight when licensed hunters were out shooting rabbits and foxes. Suitably chastened, I didn't dare mention that I had a cat on a leash with me or retort that neither foxes nor rabbits carried torches on their nocturnal wanderings.

Well, after that I thought, I wonder what the locals will make of it; perhaps someone could cast some light on the matter. With this in mind I joined the throng of regulars at the Northumberland Arms which nestles at the foot of the bank down the road from our cottage. Glass of wine in hand, I recounted my tale to a group of habitual drinkers at the bar whom I knew had lived in the area for most of their lives. The end of my account was greeted by a stunned silence. Then the whole group, including the barmaid whom I had expected to be more sympathetic, broke into peals and guffaws of laughter. Shocked by their reaction I demanded to know what there was to laugh about. It was several minutes before the roars and chuckles of merriment subsided sufficiently for anyone to give me an answer. Then in broad Geordie accent I was told, 'Well, you know, you go out in the middle of the night for a walk in the woods and, worse still you take your pet cat with you; it is no wonder somebody took a shot at you. They probably thought you were a lunatic or a werewolf!'

More hilarity followed. Aware that my dignity had been severely compromised I managed a rueful grin and accepted several friendly slaps on the back as gracefully as I could manage. Joan the barmaid asked how big my cat was, a question that aroused another bout of hysterical laughter. Desperate not to appear a complete idiot I told them he was a Maine Coon and about as big as a Yorkshire terrier but anything I said simply made them erupt in giggles and sniggers. When I looked round at the group, some had laughed so much that their faces were tear-stained. I felt I couldn't win and made to leave but they prevailed upon me to stay. Somebody bought me a drink and gradually the mirth subsided and I was able to make my escape accompanied by jestful remarks such as 'Remember to keep your head down!'

Once outside I was joined by Derek, who had worked as a gamekeeper and water bailiff, and he explained to me that gangs from the city areas came up to the river at night using nets to poach fish, trout and salmon, which they then sold from the back of a van on the black market around the backstreets and to some restaurants in the Newcastle and Gateshead areas. It was big criminal business and in the past water bailiffs had been attacked and injured. The police had a file on it but nothing much seemed to have been done. It was probable that those people who shot at me mistook me for a game warden or bailiff and were determined to frighten me off to avoid arrest.

'Well they certainly succeeded,' I said.

'You'd best steer clear of the river at night,' Derek said. 'Sometimes they've been known to bring big dogs with them. If you want a walk at night go down to the coast; it's a lot safer!'

And with that he bade me goodnight and went on his way and I reflected with horror on what he had told me. I realized that Pablo, by abruptly stopping, had saved us from a fate too terrible to contemplate.

I returned home in sober mood and indulged Pablo with lots of strokes and endearments. I informed him that there would be no more midnight walks in the woods by the river. He stared at me gravely as if to say, 'I second that!'

The experience in the woods by the river that night had given me much cause to ponder the changing world in which we now lived, so different in essence from the beloved England into which Toby Jug had been born and raised over thirty years earlier.

When he reached the age of six months we took Pablo to the vet's to be neutered. I hated to do that to him but it was regulation for pedigree cats and it also meant that he wouldn't wander miles away to pair up with female cats in heat and have to fight off other tom cats for the opportunity to mate with a she-cat. Whenever any of my cats need to be taken for veterinary procedures I find it an anxious time, whatever the treatment might be. I know it is possibly an irrational response but accidents do happen and I am always worried until my cats are back with me safe and sound. So it was with Pablo. I took him at the arranged time and left him. He looked at me nervously on leaving and I knew that he would be fretting because he had not been fed that morning on vet's orders, as he was to be given a general anaesthetic. I was told to come back in two hours during which time I nervously drank coffee in a local cafe and attempted to read my newspaper.

When I went back to collect him there was a most awful din going on in the surgery, mainly caused by several dogs barking, especially one large and vicious-looking German Shepherd which appeared to be trying to escape his lead and attack some other dogs waiting there. No one appeared to be in control as I approached a harassed-looking young receptionist sitting in front of a computer. I asked her if she knew anything about my cat. She told me she didn't but she mentioned there had been several emergencies during the morning but hadn't heard whether a cat was involved. After hanging around for several more minutes I began to feel really concerned and this information from the receptionist had done nothing to mitigate my apprehensions. So without any further hesitation I charged into the inner sanctum of the surgery to be confronted by a tall gaunt woman dressed for the outdoors in muddy green wellies and smelling of cowsheds and farm animals.

'I am looking for my cat; he's in here to be neutered,' I ventured in the face of her inquisitorial stance.

'Please return to the waiting room and your cat will be returned to you!'

I was not to be so easily placated but tried to remain polite. 'My cat has been here for almost three hours; I am worried about him and want him back now!' I said forthrightly.

Just then, before the moment of confrontation could develop into a more serious exchange, the tousle-haired figure of a veterinary nurse appeared in the corridor and exclaimed: 'Oh, Dr O'Connor, your cat is now ready for collection. Please follow me and I'll show you the way.'

Avoiding the haughty and disapproving stare of the woman vet in the smelly wellies, I hurried to catch up to the nurse. 'Had a busy day?' I asked as we strode together down the passage.

'It's been like World War Two!' she said, grimacing, but later managed a smile.

We entered a cubicle where, safe in his carrying box, lay Pablo, smelling strongly of anaesthetic. He gave me a mournful look that said: 'Do you know what they've done to me?' Sighing with relief at the sight of him alive and well, I thanked the nurse and carried him out of the bedlam of the waiting room to the car. All the way home I praised him and promised to personally look after him for the rest of the day.

When we arrived at the cottage Catherine was waiting for us and gave Pablo some very gentle hugs and lots of words of welcome, but probably equally important from his point of view was that she had his dinner and bowl of biscuits ready for him. Although he appeared at first to be somewhat groggy, our growing cat, who seemed to be getting bigger every day, soon became his normal self. Sniffing and sneezing at the scents of the medication on his skin, he gave himself a thorough tongue-wash and then relaxed on a window sill in the sunlight.

During the days that followed his operation Pablo seemed to want to be closer to us than ever before, probably as a reaction to the trauma of being separated from us as well as the procedure itself. Cats are capable of storing memories and the emotions aroused cause them to feel vulnerable long after the actual event. This is why Pablo needed some extra loving from us to tide him over the experience.

He loved to play with us so when he pulled himself together we played together often. We had bought him a number of cat toys which he tended to play with during the night when he was alone in the conservatory. Often we could hear him racing around and jumping about. In the morning we would find his toys strewn around, well-bitten and torn. But he preferred to play with us.

Catherine had bought a brightly coloured cloth bird which was attached to the end of a stick by a piece of elastic. When we waved it about in front of Pablo the result would be the most extraordinary display of acrobatics, including outstanding leaps, bounds and twists of his body whilst airborne. But Pablo's preferred form of play was a rough and tumble with me. This usually involved me grabbing him and rolling him about on the floor whilst trying to avoid his big sharp claws. Another thing he enjoyed was when I ran along the hallway with him in hot pursuit, grabbing and biting at a trouser belt which I trailed behind me. These activities usually escalated to the point where he would wrench the belt from my hold, tear upstairs with it in his mouth and then lie on the top landing waiting for me to mount a counter move. Usually, I was the one who ended up exhausted and, much to Pablo's disappointment, would retire hurt with several scratches requiring medication and needing a rest.

Once Pablo was allowed to roam free, I would play this game

with him in a modified form out in the garden where I would run about trailing a length of rope behind me with him furiously chasing me. One day this playtime ended in a shock trauma for him when he sped off with the end of the rope in his mouth and me running after him; he made a detour over the compost heap where a cutting from a rose bush became entangled in his fluffy tail. Unable to free himself from it he panicked, dropped the rope and raced away into deep undergrowth to hide. I was convulsed with laughter at this turn of events but Catherine, who had been watching from the kitchen window, was more sympathetic and hurried to the aid of the terrified cat. Removing the offending branch from his tail she carried him into the cottage for treats and sympathy. Later, I received a deserved scolding. Following some soothing strokes from Catherine and after consuming a mouthful of tasty treats, Pablo was once again ready for action, cried to be let out and ran to join me. He didn't seem much bothered by his recent scare but for the sake of our continuing good relations I offered him my apology for laughing at him. Cats hate to be laughed at and go into a great huff when it happens, but in this case Pablo seemed more interested in resuming play. To please him we did a few more run-arounds before I called it a day and we retired indoors for tea and relaxation.

Generally, Pablo soon recovered his aplomb following situations like the one above and in a short while played as enthusiastically as ever. Because he liked both or at least one of us to join his games, he developed strategies to ensure that we did. When he became bored he resorted to a number of antics to attract our attention. These included knocking the telephone off the hook; thudding his body against the sitting room door; and clinging by his claws to the top of the opening door to hitch a ride. If these tactics didn't work then he would charge up to us with a ball or piece of ribbon in his mouth. He also loved to race upstairs via the wooden banister and then hurl himself back down in leaps and bounds. None of this does any good for the furnishings and decor, of course, but Pablo was so lovable and dependent on us that we could not resist just hugging him and even encouraging him so that we could laugh at his clowning around the cottage.

But Maine Coon cats, especially the males, tend to grow very large as they mature and once they become heavier the possibility for destructive rumbustious behaviour becomes alarmingly evident. The problems caused by a kitten running helter-skelter through the house can be bad enough but a burly Maine Coon with an abundance of energy can do considerable damage to the happy home. As Pablo grew bigger he needed to learn some discipline and, since his breed is noted for its intelligence and willingness to please, it was not difficult with patience to teach him acceptable behaviour in our cottage.

It is worth describing the first day that he was old enough to be let out by himself because it illustrates the true nature of his character. At first he just stood as if rooted to the spot. Then he turned and looked at me as if to say, 'Why aren't you coming?'

'Go on, enjoy yourself. You're a big lad now and you're free!' I said to him.

Eventually he moved off, if somewhat diffidently. I turned and went back inside the cottage for a cup of coffee and to hear the news on the radio. Suddenly, Catherine called me from the conservatory. 'Come and see Pablo; you must not miss this!' I hurried outside into the garden and abruptly became aware of a terrific clamour coming from a copse of tall trees at the edge of our garden. 'Can you spot him? Look, there he is!' she said pointing to the said trees.

And then I caught sight of him high in the topmost branches of an ash tree; he was swaying back and forth as he fought to maintain his balance. The clamour was being caused by a crowd of rooks who were noisily buzzing him. For his part Pablo was trying to retaliate by swiping out with his huge paws at the circling birds. 'Don't think I'm afraid of you lot!' he seemed to be saying, as far as I could make out. The sight of him swinging around in the spindly branches, his bronze and sable-coloured fur gleaming in the morning sunlight, was for me a foretaste of the way in which Pablo's personality would emerge as 'the wild cat within' and increasingly come to dominate his life. Regrettably, this would eventually result in his death but for the present we shared his joy at being free.

'Should we go and call him down?'

'No,' I said. 'He's only having fun. Let's leave him be.'

With that said we both went back into the cottage, although Catherine kept going to the window and anxiously looking into the garden to see what he was up to.

Later, Pablo gave us both a scare because he did not return

that night. Around midnight I took my large-beamed lantern and, at Catherine's urgent request, went to look of our missing big cat. I searched the garden, called, whistled and shone my light all around the trees and hedgerows adjacent to our property, but of Pablo there was no sign. I must admit that at this stage I wasn't worried unduly. As I explained to Catherine, it was a warm summer night and there were a lot more interesting things for a cat to investigate than thoughts of home. But we were both showing signs of parental concern at our missing child substitute.

In the morning all apprehension was relieved by the appearance at the conservatory door of a bedraggled Pablo whining loudly to be let in. As I moved to open the door, Catherine called from upstairs telling me not to do so as she could see from the window a row of rodent bodies lying on the patio. Obviously, Pablo had been hunting through the night and was the perpetrator. Catherine didn't want him carrying any of his kills inside the cottage.

'It's OK,' I called back. 'I'll grab him and lift him in.' Opening the door in one quick motion, I reached down and grasped Pablo around his middle, hauling him indoors whilst slamming the door shut. He stared up at me as if to say, 'Have you seen what I caught for you? Aren't I clever?' after which, head held high, he trotted proudly towards the kitchen for his breakfast to be followed, no doubt, by a well-deserved cat nap.

Meanwhile, there remained the problem of the line of rodent corpses outside. 'If we don't get rid of them he might start to eat them and be sick!' said Catherine, who was surveying the dead bodies.

'It's alright,' I said. 'I know what to do. I've been here before.'

And memories flooded back of all the times over the years I had needed to surreptitiously dispose of dead mice and voles before my cat became aware of what I was doing. As I set to clearing away the rodent corpses another more poignant memory came back to me which involved a different cat and an earlier but happy time in my life.

I recalled an incident that took place in Owl Cottage when Toby Jug was about two years old. I was busy in the kitchen when I heard some strange noises coming from another room. When I went in to investigate I was confronted by a strange sight. Toby Jug was standing, body arched, rigid on all fours, in a hunched crouch, staring at something by the fireplace. Worse still, he was making hissing and spitting sounds which I had never heard from him before. It was February and the room, having no lights switched on, was in semi-darkness. I strained to see what was arresting Toby's attention. Something moved in the shadows by the fireplace, eliciting a throaty growl from Toby Jug. At once I spotted it – the largest mouse I had ever seen. Surely it must be a hybrid, I thought. But what struck me as most bizarre of all was that the creature was baring its teeth and making muted snarls in the direction of Toby. I assumed that this was a developing situation which could only end one way and that was by Toby Jug killing this rather obnoxious-looking rodent. In order not to precipitate the matter I withdrew to allow what my medical friends term 'a therapeutic wait', wherein things can change for the better without further intervention. It was after five o'clock and, since I had been working hard in the kitchen, I poured myself a glass of claret, sat down in an easy chair and awaited the outcome.

When I checked, the stalemate was still ongoing: it was what you might call a 'Mexican Standoff'. From my vantage point beside the door I came to the conclusion that Toby was afraid to attack; he didn't know what to do. After all, he hadn't ever had an experience of killing anything since his mother had died before she had the opportunity to train her kitten in life skills for cats. Well, I thought, it is beyond my capabilities to emulate a female cat in respect of hunting and killing a mouse, however urgent it is for Toby to learn. He'll have to learn some other way. With that, I charged into the room and scared the big mouse away. I noticed, in the receding daylight, as it bounded and leapt away, that it had a patch of brown fur over its black back, like a cloak, unlike most house mice, which have grey fur. This gave it a most sinister look. Furthermore, it had very pronounced ears that were roundel-shaped like those of Walt Disney's Mickey Mouse. This thing was a monster, no doubt about that. I watched it exit through a hitherto unnoticed crevice in the stone wall of the room and told myself that I would need to give that some attention as soon as possible.

Next, I turned my focus on Toby Jug and picked him up. I got the feeling that he needed a cuddle because he'd suffered something of a shock. 'You and me both, pal,' I said, adding, 'You've a lot to learn yet, though; don't worry too much about it for the present.' Several times that evening Toby went to the gap in the stone wall where the mouse had gone through and gave it a thorough investigative sniff as well as several fierce hisses. 'Don't distress yourself!' I told him. 'Tomorrow we will go to a shop I know in Rothbury where I can buy just the thing to deal with Mr Mouse.'

After breakfast the next morning I set off in my white Mini for the rural market town of Rothbury, with Toby Jug catnapping on the front passenger seat. The town was bustling with early shoppers as I parked opposite the butcher's shop, famous throughout the area for game and special-recipe luxurious sausages. The shop I wanted was some distance up the sloping street and so, leaving Toby in the car, I crossed the road, trying to ignore the inviting smells of freshly made meat pies emanating from a home bakery, and headed for the store which had the local nickname 'The Old Curiosity Shop', after Dickens'. Inside the store it was gloomy and there was just one light bulb hanging above the counter for illumination.

The glum expression of the proprietor matched the dingy interior of the shop but it purported to stock every hardware item you might want.

'What are you after, then?' he grunted in a far from welcoming manner.

'I would like a "live" mousetrap. Even two if you have them, please,' I added politely. The vehemence of his response surprised even me although I was aware of his irascible reputation.

'It's only fools that would want to keep rodents alive. What you should have are killer traps or poison,' he said, glaring at me.

'Do you have any humane traps for sale?' I persisted.

He sighed, gave me another hard look, then muttered, 'There might be a few left of the ones bought in for the nuns at Lemmington Hall. What are you wanting to do, train them to sit up and beg?' With this last rejoinder he came as near as he could to smiling, only it wasn't a smile; it was more of a sneering smirk. Then he disappeared into the dim interior of the store. Several minutes later he reappeared carrying two lengthy wooden boxes with wire trap-doors at each end, all covered in dust and cobwebs. 'These will have to do for you,' he said ungraciously. 'That will be four shillings for the both of them.'

I paid him without further comment and with a cheerful 'cheerio' left the shop, stopped to buy two hot meat pies at the bakery and rejoined Toby Jug. He was sitting waiting inside the car on the shelf of the rear window and attracting curious stares, sometimes smiles, from passersby.

'We'll soon be home,' I told him as he leapt to my shoulder and purred all the way on the drive back. 'I've got us a pie each for lunch!' I said. At this, his purrs resonated even more loudly. Maybe he couldn't understand my words but he could obviously smell the pies and put two and two together. Smart cat.

When we arrived back at the cottage I examined the traps. They were rather scruffy but I thought that might be an advantage in luring the mouse into one since a clean trap with my scent all over it might make it wary and I really wanted to catch the creature. Toby, true to his nature, was full of curiosity and watched my every move. First, I rubbed the inside of the trap with a piece of cheese to awaken the mouse's interest and then I put two cubes of cheese inside the trap. I did the same with the second trap and set them ready. I placed them along the wall where the mouse had made his exit and awaited developments, although I realized that it would probably be sometime in the middle of the night before the trap would be sprung. That is, if our adversary deigned to appear.

Then, after giving my hands a good wash to clean them after handling the traps, I turned my attention to our lunch. Cutting Toby's pie in half, since a whole one would be far too much for him, I set his tray down for him. By the time I had served up a mixed salad with the pie for myself, Toby Jug had consumed his in double-quick time and was now busy licking gravy stains off his lips and preparing to give himself a tongue-wash.

In the afternoon I attended to some chores of the tidying-up variety around the garden. Toby Jug sat in his favourite old apple tree and I could tell from his expression as I glanced towards him occasionally that something was bothering him. It didn't take me long to guess that he was still worried about the mouse he should have caught yesterday. Later, while I relaxed with a book and a drink in front of the fire, Toby Jug couldn't settle and kept pacing back and forth around the traps, wondering what might be going to happen.

'Time for bed,' I said, and headed up to the bedroom followed by a cat who appeared to be in two minds as to whether to go to bed or stay on guard downstairs, ready to confront the mouse. After an uneventful night we rose in the morning and I set about preparing breakfast only to find that Toby Jug was nowhere in evidence. On hearing a scraping sound from the sitting room I hastened to investigate. The sight that greeted me took me by surprise even though it was half expected.

Toby was circling one of the traps, which had been sprung. Even more surprising than this quick result was the fact that the trap was being continually bounced over the floor by the creature inside. It was banging and crashing against the doors of the trap, trying to burst out. But the big mouse was well and truly captured. I picked up the trap to view the captive. The first impression I had was of a very large rodent unlike the small grey and brown creatures I was accustomed to seeing around the garden and driveways. It was a male and he looked ferocious. He glared back at me and recommenced thrusting against the trap door that had him imprisoned.

'Right,' I said. 'The sooner we get rid of you the better for all of us. Come on, Toby – we've a journey to make.'

Wasting no time I backed the car out of the garage and was quickly joined by a curious cat who was determined to see this through even though he had not yet had his breakfast, which normally would have been an immediate priority. We had a monster mouse to deal with. I placed the trap with the mouse into a shopping bag and put it on the floor of the car by the passenger seat, watched all the while by a bemused if somewhat apprehensive cat.

The informed rural advice regarding how far to take captive rodents before freeing them was about two miles; this was to ensure that they did not return to the place where they were caught. With this in mind I drove several miles down the A1 and turned off on the outskirts of Tarbrook Farm. Leaving Toby Jug in the car I took the trap to the border of a leafy lane overgrown with weeds and levered it open. After a moment's hesitation the mouse hurtled out into the coarse grass for a short distance then, amazingly, stopped, turned, raised itself upright and glared back at me, chittering like an angry squirrel before disappearing into a darkened ditch. To say the least, I was dumbfounded. I had never seen anything like it.

As I walked back to the car I smiled at the sight of Toby glued to the windscreen so he could witness proceedings. He seemed relieved to see the back of the little beast, but no more than I was. Later that day, I decided to address the problem of the hole in the wall, through which I'd seen the mouse leaving. From the greenhouse I brought a smoke bomb which was used to fumigate the place at the end of the season. Now, returning indoors, I lit the blue fuse end, pushed it into the wide crevice and then taped it into position. Next I went outside in the garden to view the other side of the wall. Sure enough a tell-tale trail of smoke was issuing forth from around a stone at the base. I chalked the spot and determined to fill the opening with cement as soon as possible. It would be a weekend job, which I thought I would probably do the next day. Whilst all this was going on I was followed about by a most interested cat who kept well away from the smoke but watched attentively from a safe distance.

Watching Toby, I was reminded of his behaviour the previous evening when he had, in a perplexed manner, kept returning to the entry crack in the wall, sniffing warily and then spitting a warning at the place where the mouse had disappeared. I suppressed a smile as I looked at him still trying to work out what he should have done when he first confronted the mouse. He couldn't quite sort it out in his mind but I knew that eventually he would when he grew and matured some more. 'Never mind Toby; I'm sure you'll have other chances to deal with mice,' I said to him lovingly.

Later that week, in a conversation with Richard Morris, my illustrator, he told me that mice of this kind were to be found in some country areas around the south of England. My intruder had obviously been a migrant. I hoped he would be the last. And so, with the thought that the past is always with us, I ended my ruminations about life with Toby Jug at least for that day and turned my attention back to the present and the disposal of Pablo's kills.

Pablo rejoiced in the opportunity he was given to wander at will and with the availability of lush woodland, open fields and river banks adjacent to the cottage he was spoilt for choice. Whilst the countryside around us mainly comprises traditional farmland there are hidden areas of wooded copse and overgrown bush-covered gullies in which wildlife thrives. In one covert domain rabbits and hares, foxes and badgers, weasels and stoats, colourful cock pheasants and partridges, redshank and woodpigeon, to mention only a few, live in secluded sanctuary. Here and there in this area you can still come across a green meadow, open to the sky but surrounded by dense foliage and tree growth which may harbour an abandoned gamekeeper's wooden shack. Not far away, there may be a tumbledown barn in which owls, swifts and swallows roosted and where poachers once took refuge. Now, such an area is the province of an itinerant population of wildlife refugees who are looking for a home to raise their young and to live peaceful lives.

Sometimes in the middle of a large field wild zones can be found which the farmer has not cultivated, possibly because it contains weighty rock mounds, or simply because he is a kind man who believes in conserving animal- and bird-life. These small plantations provide precious habitats for flora and fauna which would otherwise be denied living space. Happily, more farmers are now being encouraged to set aside land for such purposes.

I know of a stretch of land nearby which is littered with scattered boulders and rock outcrops, fringed with self-setting saplings and overgrown with broom and brambles. It provides an ideal environment for numerous small species of mice and shrew, as well as ground-nesting birds such as the skylark, to breed and flourish. In a dip in the land there is a drainage ditch which has been left undrained and, fed by the rains, it has grown into a pond providing suitable conditions for eels and exotic-coloured newts to thrive, as well as iridescent dragonflies and damselflies which flit and hover around the water's edge like vibrant humming birds. In time, coots and moorhens will most probably take up residence here and in a short while the area will be a thriving wildlife habitat. While wandering around such an environment, Pablo will be perfectly at home; it is, after all, his natural-born heritage as a cat.

In the early days of Pablo's life with us, like any pet owners we had to learn to accommodate him and he, us. For Pablo this involved accepting the need to treat the carpets, curtains and furniture with a certain amount of respect and to acknowledge the need for hygienic toilet practices. For our part, life with Pablo demanded a tolerant attitude to his preference for leaving animal and bird carcasses at the back door as offerings to us on a very regular basis. It also required forbearance towards a drenched presence plaintively wailing for entry after a stormy night spent hunting in the woods and fields. After his expeditions we would often have to spend time cleaning him up, drying him off and picking the burrs and thistle heads from his tangled fur. Pablo would look up at us and sigh as if to say, 'Well, you know all this is what cats have to do.' The process was a two-way track. We sought to teach him about our way of life and he encouraged us to understand and participate in the ways of the wild and the way of the cat.

As the evening developed into darkness Pablo would come to me and indicate that it was time for a prowl. He would signal this by raising himself on his back legs and padding his paws up and down on the glass door of the conservatory. When I opened the door, and just before he made his exit, he would usually turn and look up at me as if inviting me to accompany him like the times in his youth when I took him for walks on his harness.

Sometimes when I am free to follow my mood I will grab my coat and torch, and tag along with him. The first time I did this was a delightful experience during which I was initiated by my Pablo into the world of the cat. I left the conservatory and found him waiting for me by the beech tree in which the ring doves build a nest each year. As I joined him he paused to give his chest a quick lick and then padded off with a purpose in mind. Excited, I followed him. Once outside the garden I couldn't see a thing. More to the point, I couldn't see Pablo.

Then I heard a familiar throaty meow and felt him brush against my leg. I got the feeling that he was intent on guiding me on a tour of his making, like a child showing a parent around his playground. He stayed behind me for some reason and then approached me from the rear as cats are wont to do. I stroked and praised him and he led me forward only for me to lose sight of him once more. I took out my torch and shone it around to see where he was. Then I spotted a startled brown furry face slightly to the side of me and suddenly realized how stupid my action had been. Artificial light at night is anathema to wild creatures; it is an unnatural abomination associated only with human kind. For the nocturnal residents of the countryside improvised light is an unwelcome intrusion which deprives them of their visual acuities and frightens everything, both predators and game, away. The experience caused me to reflect. Here am I in the outdoors at night, an outsider divorced from the natural ways, by reason of being 'civilized'. My cat's senses of hearing and smell, as well as his vision, are infinitely superior to mine and without the trappings of my domesticated environment I can no longer lay claim to belong to the natural environs which initially bred humanity. This was a sobering thought. In this setting, I was inferior to my cat and just about every animal that lived out there.

I found Pablo lying some distance in front of me in a crouched pose, intent on something out there in front of us. He acknowledged my presence as I joined him with the merest flick of his tail, which is a cat's way of responding to someone without breaking concentration.

We were situated at the edge of a mown hayfield which extended a vast distance over rolling landscape. Pablo lay motionless, nose and ears twitching now and then with the scents and sounds wafting over the soft autumn breeze. This was his method of reconnoitring the ground over which he would soon be moving. At last he turned and looked at me, and made an affectionate throaty sound. 'Can you understand what I see and hear and scent?' These were his unspoken queries. His bright eyes, shining like huge emeralds in the light from the moon, implored my comprehension. I struggled mentally to appreciate what he was experiencing and the quality of it. Suddenly, in a burst of intuition I became aware of what my Pablo was thinking and feeling. I strove to fine tune the meanings flowing between us.

'See how the grasses flow before the wind, hiding the creatures I would hunt. I can scent rabbit and partridge. There are field mice and shrews; I can hear them eating worms and scrunching beetles. Over by the fringes of the wood I hear bats fluttering and squeaking as they make ready to fly off to hunt. On a branch of the oak I can see the little owl waiting to pounce.'

Such a rush of perceptions stunned me and left me blank. I could see and hear nothing of it. To me it was just darkness and silence except for the sighing of the wind. Then the moon emerged from behind the clouds and blanched the landscape. Pablo glanced up at me in farewell and then, with innate stealth, he faded into the rippling grasses with no more than a hint of shadow. He had left to follow the call of the wild.

I felt a sense of loss at his going, a lonesome feeling that I took away with me as I retraced my steps homewards. He left me because he knew at that point of time that I was incapable of entering and sharing his world either physically or mentally. I just couldn't tune in and match his natural-born prowess.

Later in the cottage, in a thoughtful mood, I reflected that with increasing human dependency on scientific technology we are losing contact with our natural origins and preventing ourselves from accessing the vast reservoir of innate knowledge which is intuitively available to us, thus forfeiting the fund of wild wisdom which is freely available to cats and other animals. Thinking about this night's experience with Pablo I became aware, not for the first time, of the cost that civilization has imposed on us. Because of this I feel myself drawn progressively closer to the domain in which my cats live and through which they function. What happened that night triggered and re-awakened a vestige of what lay dormant within me. I retired to bed with these thoughts on my mind and with the hope that in the morning when I came downstairs and drew back the curtains the first thing I would see would be Pablo, safe and sound, waiting to be let in.

Pablo was affectionate and responsive to our overtures to tame and discipline him but yet he retained the right to fulfil his origins as a cat. He was usually quiet and withdrawn in his manner and temperament, and became more so as he matured and did his own thing. If he was a human being we would probably call him introverted. Whilst we adored Pablo and he obviously loved us, he could at times appear remote, totally engrossed in his own world.

In reading through a cat book I saw some photographs of silver-grey Maine Coon cats who were purported to be outgoing and dashing. Perhaps Pablo, I thought, was missing the company of his own kind and another cat, a playmate, would bring him out a little more satisfactorily for them both.

Pablo will return to our story later, but first I want to begin to tell the tale of our first silver-grey Maine Coon, an interesting and remarkable character, whose friendship did just what I wanted for Pablo and who initially brought chaos into our reasonably well-ordered lives.

CARLOS

'He's one in a million,' Jane said to me over the phone. 'I could have sold him many times over as soon as I put the pictures of his litter up for sale on my website. But he's all yours if you still want him. He's five weeks old now so you can come and see him. What would you like his pet name to be?'

'Carlos!' I said, the jubilation rising within me. I had been speaking to Jane, the Maine Coon breeder from whom we had bought Pablo. For the reasons I gave above I had contacted Jane and discovered that she had recently sent her silver she-cat Florence to be mated with a superb silver stud called Oscar. The litter had duly arrived and her phone call to me was about one of the kittens who was a striking silver-grey in colour.

Of course, all kittens look appealing but he was exceptional. The first time I saw him I was truly amazed. He was the most beautiful kitten I had ever seen and I loved him at first sight; a tiny fluffy ball of silver fur with a baby round head, minute pointed ears and piercing blue eyes that held a sparkle of intelligent depth about them. He was irresistible.

But there was something else about him that I could not at first identify; then it came back to me. It happened when I was on holiday in Zimbabwe. One day I had visited an animal sanctuary where injured animals and orphans of the bush were fostered until they could fend for themselves again. What I saw in the eyes of a leopard cub, which snarled at me, was also there in the eyes of my new kitten, Carlos. It was an almost indefinable wild glint of life from the jungle depths which Rudyard Kipling had ventured to describe in *The Jungle Book*. 'He's been here before!' exclaimed Jane knowingly, nodding towards the kitten nestling contentedly in my arms.

The next time I saw him he was ten weeks old. In another two weeks I would be able to bring him home but I just had to see him again. The regulations governing pedigree Maine Coons, as indeed with most other pedigrees, stated that kittens had to be three months old with all their health jabs before they could be allowed to join the new owners. Carlos didn't disappoint me. He was so full of life that he could hardly stay still even for a moment. He impressed me as being a little cat with a big mission. He seemed determined to investigate everything in his world that came even remotely into his line of vision. And these things, whatever they were, had to be explored robustly and at full gallop, which inevitably caused chaos in Jane's house.

One particular incident led to a medical emergency. Carlos had been playing chase games with some of the other kittens when it all got out of hand. He was on the top of the stairs when in a state of mega-excitement he took a flying leap through the banister rails, missed the kitten he was aiming at and crashed into the wall halfway down. He rolled to the bottom of the stairs and lay still.

Fortunately, Jane was on hand to witness this leap and its consequences. She was horrified. Suspecting that Carlos might be seriously injured she wrapped him in a towel, rushed to the car and drove as fast as she could to the vet's. Charging into the consulting room she pleaded for him to be examined immediately as a matter of emergency. As the duty veterinarian unwrapped the towel, Carlos, looking decidedly dizzy, was just beginning to regain consciousness. To Jane's relief he was unhurt or damaged in any way, just a trifle shocked and shaken. During the rest of the evening he was moderately calm and restful, which gave the rest of the cat family, as well as Jane and Dave, a peaceful respite. She was quick to inform me of this incident and the outcome but she was also anxious to mention that she was praying for the time when he would come to me.

'So am I,' I told her.

When I told Catherine of this latest episode in the riotous life of our new kitten she remarked: 'Well, you wanted a commando and now you've got one.'

Thinking back to that time, I can recall that look in the eyes of Carlos, how lucid and startling they were in a savage and primitive but most appealing way. Looking at his photographs as a kitten I am instantly reminded of the saying that the eyes are the mirror of the soul. The eyes of Carlos held more than a hint of the wilderness in him.

It was a warm sunny day in early July when Carlos at last came to us. To look at, he was a veritable picture, the iconic chocolate box image. But his behaviour quickly made a shambles of our careful preparations for his arrival and at times bedlam reigned. I soon began to realize that Carlos, beautiful as he might be, was suffering a hyperactive condition to an extreme degree; he was blatantly out of control and in grave need of remedial training. The evidence for this became only too apparent the first night after he had arrived. Catherine had retired early to bed and had taken Carlos up with her in an attempt to calm him down. Suddenly, she appeared in the sitting room where I was watching television. She exclaimed helplessly, 'I can't deal with this kitten. He is completely out of control.' This statement, coming from an experienced education professional in the field of disruptive and deviant behaviour, caused me no end of alarm and I swiftly realized that a state of emergency was developing in our normally tranquil household!

It appeared that on entering the bedroom, Carlos had proceeded to rip the plush velvet headboard and began to tear ferociously at Catherine's Egyptian cotton pillow cases. Then he had raced around the top of the walls via the expensive embossed wallpaper and finally he had flung himself headlong at the fragile curtains at one of the windows, ripping them to shreds. This was all in the space of a few minutes and from a tiny little chap no bigger than a bunny rabbit. Catherine had at last managed to grab him and, furious at the havoc he had caused, angrily thrust him into my arms. 'You'd better deal with him or back he goes,' she said determinedly.

After his rampage upstairs Carlos came to me all sweet and

loving, purring like mad as I held him up to face me to give him a stern ticking off. By chance a stray strand of hair fell down on my forehead just as I was giving him a really hard talking to. Unable to resist the temptation he took a playful swipe at it and scratched me across the bridge of my nose, all in fun, at least from his point of view.

'That's it,' I cried, and stalked outside with him and shut him in the garden woodshed. 'Let's see what a spell of solitary confinement will do to your attitude,' I shouted at him. Then I retired to the bathroom for medication.

'Did you manage to sort him out dear?' Catherine called down from the bedroom. I ignored her as male pride would not allow me to answer. It was plain to see that Carlos would require all my skills as a psychologist and cat lover if there was to be any effective sorting-out to be done.

I left him in the woodshed for twenty minutes before I went out to fetch him. All the neighbourhood dogs were barking their heads off, even the distant ones, and I soon saw why. A stream of banshee like wails was issuing from the shed holding Carlos captive. I did not know whether or not he was in pain. Had he cut or impaled himself on one of the tools in there? In my anxiety I rushed to open the door and peered worriedly into the dark interior. The wailing ceased immediately. Then I saw him, a stumpy little figure all covered in cobwebs and sawdust. He darted out and I clutched hold of him. He gave a tiny kitten meow and immediately began to purr loudly. In moments he fell fast asleep in my arms.

I resolved to go out the very next day to buy him a kitten harness in order to begin to restrain and discipline him. For now, lying blissfully asleep on my lap, he presented a picture of baby cat innocence but I decided that I would have to be firm and not let him fool me or I might lose this kitten, who I had already begun to love.

At bedtime it was decided to lodge Carlos in the conservatory, with Pablo for company. Pablo wasn't very happy about this since he preferred to go out at night, but we thought it would only be for a short while and Pablo might be a good influence on the kitten. We were delighted to find that this arrangement worked. Although Pablo snubbed and spat on first acquaintance with the new kitten, Carlos appeared to ignore such rebuffs and at bedtime was able to overcome the older cat's aloofness by simply cuddling up to him and refusing to budge. Eventually Pablo, who had a gentle heart, allowed the little cat's perseverance to prevail.

The following morning I was sitting happily at the breakfast table awaiting my bacon and eggs and Carlos was gleefully chasing a table tennis ball around the floor with feline abandon. As Catherine handed me my food, a silver streak of fur, claws and jaws erupted onto the table via my leg and made off at speed with a rasher of my bacon in his mouth. This spur-of-the-moment, opportunistic raid left me flabbergasted at the alacrity with which it had been accomplished.

'Right! That's enough. He is not getting away with that, kitten or no kitten.' And at that Catherine charged after Carlos.

Several moments later I became aware of a series of bumps and thuds from the bedroom upstairs. Feeling obliged to offer re-inforcement to what I expected to be a one-sided contest, I entered the bedroom. I was right. There I found Catherine lying full length on the floor with one hand under the wardrobe groping behind a line of her shoes. 'Got you!' she cried triumphantly as she dragged out a squirming kitten and handed him over to me.

'To the woodshed?' I ventured.

'At once,' she exclaimed. Of the stolen bacon there was no sign.

After the culprit had been locked away we resumed breakfast and held a council of war. The upshot of our deliberations was that Carlos should be restrained for at least part of the day by a harness and lead. And it was further decided that a consultation with the vet might help. Returning him to Jane for resale was, to my relief, not mooted at this stage.

As I drove up to Alnwick to purchase a suitable harness and lead for Carlos and to make an appointment at the vet's, I thought about what the best course of action was likely to be. What would be the best way to cope with our wilful kitten and curb his hyper energy? Eventually, an idea began to take shape in my mind, which I culled from my memories of my life with Toby Jug. It would be a solution requiring a lot of time and effort on my part but it might just work. In my heart I believed it had to, because I loved Carlos despite his aberrations and I could not bear to think of losing him.

It was a scruffy, dishevelled mini cat that greeted me when I opened the shed door on my return. Carlos hadn't been in the shed very long but he appeared to be contrite and immediately commenced rubbing himself against my sweater, with arched back and erect stub of a tail. Then he began an elaborate feline paw-padding rhythm that tore strands of wool from my jumper, but I must say I welcomed his attention and did not mind at all about the damage to my sweater. I guess he reminded me all too much of Toby Jug, who did the same thing.

I picked him up and held him close but not too close to my nose, just in case. I told him that from my point of view all was forgiven although I couldn't speak for Catherine. I reminded him that he was now part of our home and that we were his family, who loved and cherished him, but he must try to behave in a more controlled fashion. He stared at me as I spoke softly to him and I could identify the intelligence in that steady look of his and hoped the meaning of my message registered. His bright eyes looking up at me just melted my heart. 'Everything is going to work out fine,' I muttered, for the sake of both of us. Only time would tell.

'When is the vet's appointment?' Catherine asked.

'Tomorrow morning at 8.30,' I replied, trying to fit a harness on to the wriggling kitten, who regarded my efforts as something of a game. At last it was fastened securely and I attached the lead. 'I thought I'd take him for an introductory walk around the garden,' I said confidently.

'Good luck,' Catherine replied.

I picked up Carlos and carried him outside. Placing him on the edge of the grass to give him a chance to get his bearings, I waited for him to move, with the lead clutched firmly in my hand. Moving his head from side to side he surveyed the bushes and trees in front of him. Perhaps he's overawed, I naively thought. At that point he took off, literally. The best way I can describe his action is to compare it to a commercial aircraft roaring down the runway at a sufficient speed for the captain to issue the command 'Rotate', that is, to give it full power to enable the plane to blast off, straight up. If you can believe a cat could fly, Carlos did. He 'rotated'. The lead was jerked from my hand as he flew up from a standing start straight into the topmost branch of a young beech. From the height of his perch up in the tree he stared down at me as if to say, 'What would you like to see me do next?'

Luckily the lead from his harness was hanging down and by pulling it gently I was able to bring him within reach and catch him. As usual with this kitten, once I had hold of him he simply began to purr and rub himself affectionately against me. In such circumstances it proved difficult even to begin to reprimand him. One could only admire his quite exceptional physical prowess. The remainder of the so-called walk consisted of me dragging him along as he lay on his side, with part of the lead between his teeth, making robust attempts to break free. From the conservatory window Catherine witnessed it all and just had to laugh.

'Well, he's your cat,' she said despairingly, 'but he's going to wear you down before he tires.'

I decided that Carlos had that most enviable of dispositions: he was quintessentially happy-go-lucky. Life was his oyster and he was determined to live it with gusto.

After an early start I arrived at the vet's right on time with Carlos safely secured in an escape-proof carrying box as I ventured into the waiting room. There were already two other people there with dogs on leads. Carlos peered at the dogs through the bars of the door to his box and the dogs stared back with ears pricked and eyes set in curious mode.

Thankfully, we were called first. In the examination room a young vet introduced himself and took the box from me, opened the door and gently lifted out Carlos, who immediately started to purr loudly. At this point the surgery door opened and one of the clerks entered with some papers for signing, leaving the door slightly ajar. I was busy looking out of the window at the trees, which obviously needed a thorough pruning, and didn't see what happened next. Suddenly, I heard the vet cry out in alarm, 'He's gone!'

'Oh my God, no!' I cried, and we all set off down the corridor in hot pursuit.

Before we reached the waiting room, which was situated at the end of the corridor, the sounds of dogs barking furiously interspersed with cries of alarm and panic-stricken shouts filled me with fear and dismay.

I was fast coming to the conclusion that when Carlos cut loose those twin devils bedlam and mayhem followed in his wake. When I at last managed to push my way through a disturbed group of people blocking the doorway, I found chairs overturned, papers scattered over the floor and two dogs, a black-and-white sheepdog and a bull terrier, standing up on their hind legs baying like hound dogs at a diminutive figure perched on top of a large display cabinet. It was Carlos. I could not begin to fathom how he had got up there but what impressed me more was how in all the noise he was calmly staring down at the dogs, their frantic owners and the rest of us with sangfroid.

Due to the commotion other vets and assistants were pouring into the room and someone was only just stopped short of pressing the fire alarm. Finally, a tall gaunt vet, wearing a Barbour coat and long green Wellingtons smeared with something smelling strongly of horse, restored a degree of order by her very presence. She was the person with whom I'd had a contretemps on the occasion of my last visit with Pablo. When she spotted me her gaze moved from authoritative to downright unfriendly. Then she caught sight of Carlos, who was watching curiously from his high vantage point. She seemed to grasp immediately that he was the cause of all this upset.

'To whom does that creature belong?' she demanded.

Wishing that the ground would open and swallow me, I gulped nervously with embarrassment and said, 'He's mine. But he's only a kitten,' I added defensively.

The answer was as condemning as it was imperious: 'Remove him at once!' she barked.

There now followed a stressful interval, whilst someone went to fetch the caretaker's stepladder, during which the atmosphere could have been cut with a knife. With the help of the young vet with whom we had the appointment, I dragged Carlos from his resting place and locked him away in his box. This I carried out under the baleful glare of the alpha female vet. I made a hasty exit but just as we were leaving I heard one of the dog owners say: 'It scratched my dog's nose and she's bleeding.'

I didn't wait to hear more but rushed to the car, put the box containing Carlos on the back seat and drove away as fast as I could. What now? I thought. There would have to be a plan B; Carlos would have to be somehow transmogrified into a more peaceable cat. But in my mind I accepted that it would fall to me, not the vets, to think up some modus operandi to domesticate Young Master Carlos. Now to tell Catherine.

After another council of war, with the culprit nestling fast asleep on my knee, and my having consumed two coffees and a large brandy, a new behaviour management plan for Carlos was agreed. The main features of the plan were that Carlos would wear his harness, if not his lead, at all times until further notice so that he could be more easily restrained as necessity required.

I also decided that I would take him on trips in the car to wild places in order to make him feel vulnerable, perhaps even overwhelmed, and therefore more malleable to training. I expected, too, that our travels together would serve to bond him closely to me and hopefully that would afford a further degree of control over him.

As I looked down at him snoozing on my knees he reminded me of one of my grandmother's expressions: 'He looked as if butter wouldn't melt in his mouth.' I had to chuckle at his antics of the morning but I needed to rid myself of the feeling that Carlos and I were performing in one of those slapstick Harold Lloyd movies. It wasn't funny anymore. Tomorrow I would take him up the coast to Bamburgh and along the rocky seashore.

Strangely enough, for the rest of the day and evening he was remarkably quiet and well behaved. I wondered whether he had been mollified by the happenings at the vet's or whether he was just saving his strength for another day.

The next day I packed some sandwiches for me and biscuits for Carlos, because he preferred biscuits to meat or other cat food. I also filled myself a flask of coffee and took water for him. To carry Carlos, I had in mind to use a newly acquired papoose, a sort of carrying pouch for little dogs, with a small blanket in the bottom, because he would not yet walk on the lead.

When I was walking he would be in the bag, lying on the blanket, with only his head peeping out. He would be secured by his harness to the bag by a keyring. When I reached somewhere that I considered safe I intended to let him out and start training him to walk on the lead. I wanted him by our association and experience together to become dependent on me. The more dependent he became the more influence I would have over him. That was the plan but Carlos, I guessed, might well have other ideas.

As we set off, Carlos had his harness on without the lead,

which I was carrying in my pocket. He seemed to enjoy exploring the inside of the car in his usual intensive manner; nothing escaped his scrutiny. As we drove along the narrow winding roads of rural Northumberland, with their many bends and twists, a route I preferred to the traffic-busy A1, boredom set in and Carlos began to whine. The whine developed into a kittenish howl. I ignored it. Unable to attract my attention he resorted to physical measures. Jumping on my knees he clambered up my sweater and swaying with the movement of the car he proceeded to complain loudly in my ear. His tiny claws were like needles sticking into my arm and shoulder but I gritted my teeth and told him things were going to be different now and he shouldn't expect to have his own way all the time. I talk to my cats just as I would to a person in the belief that they somehow pick up my meaning.

He kept up his aggravations until at last we passed through Seahouses and the majestic outline of Bamburgh Castle appeared on the horizon. 'Now the fun really begins,' I muttered for the benefit of both of us. Carlos momentarily desisted from his whining as a low-flying flock of seagulls flew across the bonnet of the car. 'Come on, let's get started,' I cried as I lifted him out of the car and carried him over the dunes and down to the beach, where I sat him on the sand.

His first response was to sniff the area all around him in some trepidation. Then he just stood and sneezed several times. Suddenly a gust of cool sea breeze that is almost always present on the north-east coast ruffled his fur and caused him to shiver.

The end result was that he climbed up to sit on my shoe, looked up at me and whined.

'None of that,' I said, trying hard to be firm. 'You are the worst-behaved kitten I have ever met, probably the worst in the whole world, and it has to stop; so it begins anew here with some training in discipline for you.' He whined again, looking up at me with big, sad eyes. 'No complaints will be tolerated. Sorry,' I said harshly, tugging at his lead and heading across the beach to some nearby rock pools filled with sea water and minute marine life that I thought might arouse his curiosity.

The stroll on the beach involved me dragging Carlos on the lead across the sand. He just lay on his side and refused to walk despite being offered inducements of biscuit treats in the same way that I had trained Pablo. However, arriving in the proximity of the first pool changed this stubborn attitude. A small bird, which had been foraging for insects amongst the seaweed strewn around the sand, flew in alarm almost into the face of Carlos.

From then on my silver boy was on constant alert as we progressed towards the rock pools and he even stood up and walked to the point of pulling me along. All at once Carlos stopped and stared, with his whole body rigid, towards some rocks. He had spied something moving below the surface of the water. Flattening his body against the smooth surface of a boulder he slid forward until he could just see over the edge directly into the pool of seawater below. I guessed that it was a small fish or crab that had caught his attention. Sure enough there were several tiny crabs scuttling around the perimeter of the pool. Then I was taken completely by surprise again, although by now I should have expected it: Carlos, in ultra stealth mode, inched further towards his quarry, shook his rump once and then leapt into the pool.

I sighed. Carlos was never one to stop and stare when he could throw caution to the wind and leap into action. Indeed, if human, he would have been a natural recruit for the SAS. Soaking wet, bedraggled but defiant, I fished him out only to find he had a small crab in his mouth. Fortunately, Carlos had grabbed it from behind and the crab's nippers were facing out in front.

'Whatever am I going to do with you?' I grumbled as I levered the crab from his mouth and dropped it back in the water, where it raced off to hide, much to the dismay of a drenched kitten who was dripping seawater all over me. Afraid that he might become ill from his dunking, I hurried back to the car, holding him inside my coat and pressed against my warm sweater. I had an idea that I thought might work. Rather than driving all the way home with him in this state I drove along the beach road to Seahouses and parked outside the Bamburgh Castle Hotel because I knew there would probably be a warm log fire in the sitting room.

I explained the situation to the perplexed receptionist who thankfully recognized me from previous visits with Catherine, when we had enjoyed the special fish and chip lunch, so she did not treat me as a crank. But it was not until Carlos poked his little wet head out from my jacket that her manner melted and, chortling with sympathetic laughter, she led me into the empty lounge where there was indeed a huge log fire in the wood-burning stove, radiating warmth.

As I was settling the wet cat down in front of the life-reviving blaze the receptionist reappeared, accompanied by the housekeeper carrying a saucer of warm creamy milk for 'the dear little kitten' and a steaming mug of coffee for me. Tired out with my exertions (Carlos did tend to wear one down with his antics), I ordered a glass of ginger beer and a hot bacon sandwich and relaxed back into one of their most comfortable antique leather armchairs. Carlos, meanwhile, having consumed the milk, was indulging in a thorough tongue-wash in front of the fire, though he had to keep spitting out the seawater taste he was licking off his fur.

Just then a group of the hotel's guests crowded in from the bar, having been informed that there was a man by the fire who had rescued a kitten from the sea. I allowed this story to grow of its own accord, as rumours tend to do, and merely nodded my acceptance of their acclamation of my heroism. I need not have bothered because the focus of their attention was on Carlos, who was being enthusiastically admired by several of the ladies, each of whom was vociferous in their offers to adopt him.

'You'd get the shock of your lives,' I muttered to myself as I witnessed the fawning adulation being heaped on Carlos. True to his cat nature, Carlos was revelling in it.

It was late afternoon when at last we left and I removed a

dry and fluffy Carlos from his adoring audience, who meant well but were beginning to irritate me. Many heartfelt thanks were extended to the kind hotel staff and eventually we drove away, leaving behind our celebrity status as well as the lovely fire. Catherine was relieved to welcome us back. We noticed however that Pablo had the air of someone who was worried about the trouble that the new kitten was causing the family. He had never caused trouble like that and we began to think he was slightly miffed that he was being largely ignored of late. Or that was what we read into his non-verbal behaviour, and I made up my mind to play with him and fuss him much more than we had done of late.

That evening as I considered the events of the day I realized that I was becoming accustomed to the aberrations of Carlos, almost as if I had come to expect him to do something outrageous. But the day had not been without value for me as I remembered the lasting pleasure of experiencing the sight of an autumnal haze shrouding the misty outline of Bamburgh Castle against the big Northumbrian sky, always a sight worth seeing. Thinking about the castle set off memories of the many times I had taken Toby Jug there and picnicked amongst the sand dunes with steak pies from the famous butcher in the village. But I could never shrug off the thought that there was a strange air of loneliness about the castle, as if it did not welcome human habitation, although many people lived there in flats despite the many tales of hauntings. For many months of the year the castle and coast is subjected to cruel north-east gales which stir up fearsome storms and yet the castle and its surrounding beach area possess an ambience which exerts a positive, therapeutic uplift to the soul of the discerning visitor. Whenever I have visited the castle and the golden sands below I feel somehow spiritually refreshed and charged anew.

That evening, I recalled the long sands of the beach below the castle in the golden light of morning as we arrived and parked the car. I hoped the day I had shared with Carlos had led to as positive an effect on him as it had on me. As for me, I was now feeling emotionally and physically drained with the effort of coping with this unusual and highly volatile kitten. As if he wished to make it up to me, he jumped on to my knee and crawled right up my sweater until he faced me. He then proceeded with accompanying purrs to lick my forehead and cheek with a tongue that felt like sandpaper. I closed my eyes and endured it, and felt cheered that at least my efforts at bonding with this crazy little chap appeared to be working. Finally, he fell asleep, snoring softly, with his head tucked under my chin. I wondered as I dozed if he'd ever grow to love me as my other cats had but then I needn't have worried because cats know how to win the hearts of humankind – they'd been doing so for thousands of years. In this state we both slept until Catherine woke us just after midnight and ushered both of us off to bed.

During the next few weeks I took Carlos with me to many of the idyllic small country villages and hamlets that are delightfully characteristic of Northumberland. We travelled to Lindisfarne, which is also known as Holy Island, where Carlos chased and hunted sandflies to his heart's contentment whilst I lazed on the beach in the late autumn sun. Another day we drove to Craster and walked (although Carlos had to be carried all the way back) by the rough, rugged coastline that leads to the ruins of Dunstanburgh Castle, its stark outline dark and forbidding against the bleak sky.

That day we found a sea bass, beached by the rough seas, which was being ravaged by gulls. I could tell Carlos was desperate to chase the birds and so I let go of his lead. This afforded a unique opportunity for Carlos to indulge a machismo charge into the fray. Unfortunately, the gulls were not impressed and simply screeched fiercely and flapped their massive wings at him. I watched his face expressing fearful uncertainty, probably for the first time in his life, and concluded it would do him the world of good. Anyway, he came running back to me with many backward glances in case he was being pursued. He's learning that the world can be a dangerous place for little cats, I thought with a smile and a certain amount of satisfaction.

Another time we explored the village of Chatton, with its charming ancient church and cemetery, and we sat outside the Percy Arms where I had a large glass of merlot and Carlos demolished a meaty sausage roll. For me the experience was made all the more exquisite because the air tasted so refreshingly healthy and clean.

One day we toured the Cheviot Valleys, always a joy to me.

Carlos caught a snake while we tramped up Langleeford Valley. It was a non-poisonous grass snake but he was exuberant with his find. He wasn't so pleased when I took the snake from him and set it free it in a damp ditch. For the remainder of our walk that afternoon Carlos trotted along without having to be urged, strong in the belief, I'm sure, that at any moment he would encounter even more fascinating creatures. He was most intimidated by a fat toad he cornered when it spat in his face before it took an enormous leap into the stream that ran close by, but Carlos was having an adventure. As I watched him protectively I saw that he was thrilled by it all, which gave me no small measure of gratification.

As we travelled around I became increasingly enamoured of Carlos with his effervescent high spirits and his joyous attitude to life. Nothing seemed to daunt his gung-ho disposition. After a while he adjusted to travelling by car and was prepared to accept the restraining harness and lead. Sometimes, if anything interesting ahead caught his attention he would almost pull me off my feet with his enthusiastic urge to investigate. Small though he was, he had abundant strength. I began to feel that my plan to train him to my way of living was beginning to work without subduing his engaging spirit and his unique individuality.

I became convinced that if I had not been retired I could never have kept this kitten, with his mercurial moods, simply because I would not have had the time to spend with him.

Whilst on our excursions I was very apprehensive about

encountering people walking dogs or even, as sometimes happened, dogs wandering alone. To protect Carlos against any attack that might occur, I always carried a stout walking stick with me. I also practised swinging Carlos by his lead and harness up into my arms where I could hide him under my coat at the first sight of any problem. It did not surprise me at all that the few times I did this, Carlos seemed to enjoy it inordinately and when put down again kept looking up at me, expecting another swing – yet another example of his sporting character.

There was, however, an occasion when both Carlos and I could have been in serious danger, not from dogs, but from the elements and my own foolhardiness. I had motored away from the A1 and driven high into the moors above Chillingham within sight of the Cheviot and the foothills. The land there is exposed, wild and craggy but it provides spectacular views over open country to the distant north-east coastline.

I left the car parked just off a narrow road and headed over the moors towards a rocky outcrop where I let Carlos, attached to me by his lead, prowl among the stony crevices and boulders. It had been sunny and warm when we set off and in such conditions it is easy to travel further than intended and to forget how quickly the weather can change for the worst in high and wide open places.

Long before the storm hit us I should have noticed the signs. As I relaxed in the warm sunlight I had been unaware of what was ominously imminent. I had with interest watched a covey of small birds, probably grouse, as they erupted from the heather near to us and headed northwards. Instead of merely admiring the way in which the flock kept tight formation and moved in smooth coordination with each other until I lost sight of them, I should have heeded the warning. Wildlife, especially birds, do not move without urgent reason. If that sign did not alarm me then the sight of a low-flying squadron of wild geese fleeing towards the safety of the reed beds bordering Lindisfarne ought to have alerted me to expect a serious change in the weather. The signs are there for those who can read them. Ignore them at your peril, as I was soon to find out. The problem arose initially from the fact that I had my back to the crags and was gazing eastwards, admiring the scenic views over the moors to the sea. The storm was over us before I turned and saw, too late, the thunderous black clouds rushing at us from the west.

Within seconds, it seemed, the sky grew ominously dark, with thick cloud formations scurrying from behind us. Suddenly, it seemed a raging storm descended on us from out of nowhere. With wind and rain tearing at us we quickly became wet and cold. The weather struck at us in such a fearsome way that I completely lost my bearings and could see neither the car nor the road. We were lost in a storm and the air was becoming icy cold. The rain turned to sleet and the wind blasted us mercilessly and so with a very subdued little cat tucked inside my coat I looked for refuge.

Cold and miserable as we both were, all that I could think of doing was to wedge myself between two outcrops and wait for the storm to pass. Then I started thinking in alarm that should the storm set in for the night, and should we be obliged to spend the night here, I hadn't told Catherine exactly where we were going and she would be worried sick.

It was now so gloomy that it was quite impossible to see where we were in relation to the rest of the moor and, more importantly, the road where I had parked the car. Just as I was verging on the edge of panic I spied a welcome sight. Headlights were approaching fast. Taking Carlos out of my coat I set him down and we both made off in the direction of the approaching car. Stumbling and slipping on the wet ground I was pulled along at speed by Carlos who could obviously see better and run faster than I could. It seemed to take an eternity to reach the road but at least I could now discern the shape of my car which had been silhouetted by the lights from the passing vehicle which soon roared past us.

Whilst busying myself starting the car and turning the heater on full blast I hadn't time to think what the occupant of the car that passed us must have thought at the sight of two bedraggled figures, a man and a cat on a lead, running across the moorland in the darkness. I had parked within a mile or two of the medieval castle at Chillingham, about which there are enough tales of ghosts and ghouls to fill a large book. No doubt the driver of the car would be able to dine out on the story which, fuelled by local imagination, would enter the annals of weird hauntings.

As the warmth from the car heater began to circulate I experienced a brief spell of shivering, which soon passed. Carlos was meanwhile wrapped snugly in the car rug and seemed to be recovering well. When I turned the car round and drove down the moor to rejoin the A1 it was an easy journey back to the cottage.

Along the way Carlos poked his head out from the comfort of the blanket, stared at the road ahead and, with a little cry, gave me a long hard look. He was no doubt wondering what all that had been about. I had to chuckle because the bemused expression on the cat's face said it all. I had embarked on our excursion with only the best intentions but I realized it had been a daft and dangerous enterprise to risk our lives on a wild and desolate moor in the vicinity of the weather systems generated by the Cheviot Hills.

Soon I felt warmer and drier and was able to give Carlos my full, caring attention. He had no doubt been frightened at the turn of events but now, snug in the blanket, he looked positively his old happy self and my strokes elicited a stream of throaty purrs.

When we arrived home and I recounted our adventure, Catherine once again gave me a stern telling-off. Quite reasonably, in this instance. And we agreed I would limit such trips now that Carlos appeared to be more disciplined in his ways. From now on training for Carlos would be home-based. What a relief! Although I must say we had enjoyed some exciting outings together which I wouldn't have missed for anything.

As we relaxed together in the sitting room that evening, with

Carlos contentedly asleep with his body stretched out over my lap, I started to think about earlier times when I had ventured into the Cheviot foothills, also with a cat. Thinking along these lines I recalled a time when, at about the same period of the year, I had been asked by the principal at the college where I taught to take over the supervision of a group of mature men and women students who were going on a weekend residential course in environmental studies at the Howtel Field Studies Centre, north of Wooler. The students already had their projects planned but their college tutor had been taken ill and someone else was needed simply to take charge and to see that all went smoothly. I agreed to go as long as I could take my cat with me. The warden in charge at Howtel gave his consent and so I was able to break the news to Toby Jug, who gathered from my demeanour that something exciting was in the offing. I could tell from his bright-eyed, attentive look that he expected that we were about to embark on another adventure.

Once at the hostel, when it was time for lights out, Toby Jug could not at first be found until I discovered him in the women students' hut where he was being petted and given treats from cheese sandwiches. The students were reluctant to let me take him but I insisted for everyone's sake. He soon bedded down at the end of my bunk and so ended our first night at Howtel. I was looking forward to the weekend because my duties were limited to overseeing student welfare, leaving me free to further explore the valleys and the riverbanks with which I was already acquainted.

After breakfast on the Saturday morning, when the students had all been deployed to their various tasks, I set off in the car with Toby Jug towards the village of Etal. The narrow twisting lanes of North Northumberland wind along green corridors bordered by tall hedgerows where, in places, overhanging trees sublimely enclose the route into a verdant tunnel, above which sunbeams filter through the canopy of foliage and gleam between the leaves.

I parked the car in front of the Black Bull Inn, which is the only remaining public house in Northumberland to have a thatched roof. It is also reputed to be haunted by the ghost of a witch who lived in the seventeenth century. Regrettably the traditional hospitality of the inn did not extend to a man with a cat. We therefore repaired to the garden of the Lavender Tea Rooms opposite the Black Bull for rest and a snack. I ordered a glass of elderflower water and a slice of the cafe speciality, lavender cake. Meanwhile Toby Jug helped himself to a drink from the dog bowl near our table and watched in bewilderment the flocks of sparrows flitting between the legs of the tables, picking up scraps. I kept a firm hold on his lead but he seemed intimidated rather than aroused at their presence. He was five years old now but he had still managed to retain an ingenuous air in relation to anything which overawed him. As for the sparrows, they hardly seemed to notice him.

After a while we left the cafe and strolled along the road between the neat rows of cottages towards the ruins of Etal Castle, at the entrance to which stood a sixteenth-century cannon painted black, a grim reminder of turbulent times past in this border area between England and Scotland. We skirted the castle because I had something special in mind that entailed a journey by the little tourist railway which ran a short distance along the river to Heatherslaw and back. On our way to the railway we followed a path that wound through woodland which, at this time of year, was thickly carpeted with bluebells, and in some patches the flowers were an appealing mauve colour. Toby appeared to be so impressed by the sight of so many flowers that I guessed he wanted to run amongst them and so, there being no dogs around, I slipped off his lead and let him go. He ran off with the kind of wild abandon that only young children and animals can generate. In a short while I whistled and called his name and he came gambolling back to me like a spring lamb. This reminded me that earlier I had noticed, opposite the village cricket ground in Etal, a field full of black curly haired sheep and lambs which were considered to be very rare and hardy; it was believed by the villagers that they had been imported from the Hebrides over a hundred years ago.

Clipping Toby Jug's lead back on, I headed down a cutting to the old-fashioned railway station with the single platform. We didn't have long to wait before the train pulled in, but the noise of the little steam engine temporarily alarmed Toby, who sought refuge behind me, which he always regarded as the safest place to be. Soon we were able to board an open-sided carriage which we had all to ourselves as there were not many other passengers. The conductor appeared and I bought my ticket, though my offer to pay for Toby Jug was declined. A kindly man, he was much taken with mirthful amazement at the sight of my cat sitting upright and perky. Once the train began to rumble along the track Toby shot me an anxious look but when I simply smiled at him and gave him a reassuring wink he settled down to enjoy the ride. He adjusted, as always, very well to this new experience and before long he was jumping from one side of the carriage to the other whilst still secured, of course, by his lead. At the gentle speed we were travelling it was possible to view the scenery all around and Toby Jug was trying to do just that so that he wouldn't miss a thing.

Arriving at Heatherslaw we left the station and followed the footpath down to the working mill beside the stream. Here organic flour was produced and was available for sale in small bags, chiefly for the interest of tourists.

The return journey was pleasantly uneventful and Toby slept, no doubt soothed by the swaying motion of the carriage. He'd had a busy day but had taken it all in his stride. We were back at Howtel just before the students returned and, while they wrote up their reports, dinner was being prepared. Toby was meanwhile making friends with anyone prepared to give him some attention and kept going from one person to another. Watching him from my seat near the window I was suddenly shocked to see him confronted by a hairy miniature Yorkshire terrier. The two animals sniffed and inspected each other with cautionary care. Then the little dog gave a half-hearted bark, which sounded like a cross between a yelp and a snort, and ran off. To my amazement Toby Jug made off after him and I relaxed as the two of them had a real good play-game of chase-me. Apparently the dog was the pet of one of the women students and her husband had come to visit with her dog. As we sat down to dinner I was delighted to see the dog, called Dooley, and my Toby Jug stretched out side by side at the foot of the large oven. They looked as if they had worn each other out and were now resting. I wasn't surprised that Toby had made friends with the dog, who was slightly smaller than himself, because he had such an affectionate nature; obviously Dooley was like-minded and until the dog left the two of them got along fine. As usual, Toby joined me at bedtime but since the night had turned unseasonably cold he later worked his way under the blankets and slept cuddled into my back.

On the Sunday morning the students were again soon away, determined to complete their studies before departure that evening. I decided to take Toby Jug for a trip across the moors that lay surrounded by the Cheviot Hills. Driving to the far end of the moor I parked the car in a viewpoint lay-by and from our high elevation looked over the unspoiled clean landscape towards the sea glistening in the sunlight many miles away.

'Let's get walking,' I said to Toby, who was outside before me and already sniffing around the peaty ground with a scattering of heather covering. But the moor was windswept that day and although it looked scenically wonderful the wind tore at us in such a hostile fashion that we soon turned back for the shelter and comfort of the car. Toby's fur had been flattened to his body by the gale and both of us had been almost swept off our feet. Once inside the car the two of us began shivering.

'And so we say farewell to the Cheviot moorland and head for warmer climes,' I quipped as I put the car into gear and drove down to the village of Chatton. The Percy Arms was open and afforded a friendly welcome after the experience of being blasted off the moor. I ordered a bowl of hot vegetable broth to warm me up and the waiter cobbled together some meat scraps from the kitchen for Toby Jug.

Chatton Village is low-lying and receives a measure of protection from the bordering hills. It is one of my favourite places partly because the air is so sweet but also because the village embodies old English rural simplicity. As Toby Jug and I strolled down the lane towards the cul-de-sac that ended at the church we passed well-tended gardens and cottages, evidence that the people here really cared about their village.

The Church of the Holy Cross, which dates originally from the late seventeenth to early eighteenth centuries, is a formidable building of rough stone with a magnificent old wooden door reinforced with iron studs. The church yard has an ancient feel to it with its huge upright gravestones, rounded and weathered, the inscriptions now largely indecipherable. There is an air of melancholy yet peaceful repose about the lichen-clad stones and tree trunks with plots of wild flowers ornamenting some of the graves. Especially prominent were some fragile wild yellow field poppies and also the red variety of the same flower. Toby Jug was eager to investigate and so I let him wander at will, secure in the knowledge that this cat was tied to me by an emotional umbilical cord that had never been, nor would ever be, severed. In one corner of the church yard a flourishing yellow broom had spilled over the wall and it seemed most fitting that pretty little yellowhammer songbirds appeared to be nesting within its dense foliage. Everywhere I looked it seemed that nature had enfolded this manmade place and made it her own.

I lingered a while longer in the warm afternoon sunlight, reluctant to abandon the tranquillity I found there but a sudden summer shower cooled the air and hastened me away. I had no sooner unlocked the car door than I became aware of a frantic scrambling as Toby Jug negotiated the church yard wall and made a mad dash for the car in case I left him behind. I had to laugh because he was already sitting waiting for me on the passenger seat before I had the door fully open.

On our return journey I drove by the imposing castle at Ford, where I was often involved in specialist courses for teachers, and recalled, with a shiver, how cold the bedrooms were in winter. When I drove into the yard at Howtel I noticed that the students had already returned and then I spotted Dooley eating from a bowl. From his vantage point on my left shoulder, Toby Jug also caught sight of him and whined to be let out of the car, no doubt to join him for another bout of hectic play. Which is precisely what happened. After a cup of tea and some sandwiches everyone was anxious to be on their way. Last to leave, I thanked the warden on behalf of the college and,

Toby Jug appeared to me in a dream.

The rooks buzzed Pablo for climbing high in the tree.

Toby Jug is confronted by a hostile, big mouse.

Carlos coolly looks down on the chaos he has caused at the vet's.

collecting my weekend bag and Toby Jug, who was looking rather forlorn since Dooley had already left, we set off for home. On arriving back at the cottage Toby Jug did his usual circuit of the garden, after an absence however brief, to check that all his familiar places were intact and he assumed his customary position high in the old apple tree from where he could survey the road, examine passersby and keep an eye on me in the conservatory. Watching him now, I felt so proud of this wonderful cat who behaved in such a familiar way with me, as if he truly believed that we were of the same family of beings and that I belonged to him as a relative. He thought that between us there were no species divisions but that we were one and the same.

Finally, I closed down my mind to these blissful yet traumatic memories and focused again on the here and the now.

Looking back at my expeditions with Carlos, my mind is tinged with happy nostalgic feelings of remembered days when he and I shared very special experiences that few cat owners would even contemplate launching into. These thoughts are mingled with much sorrow that Carlos, exceptional cat that he was, is no longer with us.

But I take comfort from those times because the strategy certainly worked. Carlos and I became so closely bonded that whenever we were in the house or garden together Catherine remarked on the fact that he stuck to me like glue. Wherever I went, he followed. He loved to join me as I pottered in the greenhouse during the spring and summer months, tending my plants. He would lie for hours in a discarded cardboard box or on a disused hessian sack (a particularly favourite spot of his) and watch my every move with his natural intensity. In response to his avid attention I would talk to him. I began to treat him like a gifted child and I remember explaining how the incredibly tiny seeds I was planting could grow into tall plants bearing luscious fruits such as exotic tomatoes and cucumbers.

Eventually, I admit it, I got somewhat carried away; I was flattered by his concentration and gave him parts of my introductory student lectures on astrophysics and psychology. Captivated by the sentience in his eyes I explained in primary-school terms the meaning of Albert Einstein's formula $E=MC^2$. Catherine overheard me one afternoon and thought that this might be going a bit far, but she was impressed by the total attention Carlos gave me. He did appear to soak it all up.

Sharing his company so intimately I concluded that Carlos had such an abundance of energy that he craved outlets for it in every situation he encountered; sometimes, as I knew only too well, it simply catapulted him into action and he couldn't help himself. I had grown to love him as one adores a brilliant and precocious child and in return he demonstrated unreserved love and affection for me.

This, to my mind, is the way it is with cats when a human being makes the effort to breach the defensive wall of reserve and independence with which cats are endowed as a birthright. Once the natural aloofness and introverted characteristics of cat personality are cracked through persistent and unconditional love and attention then the cat is yours for life. Given these conditions the cat in question will lavish you with affection and that rarest of emotional attributes: dedicated attachment. This is what I was now receiving from Carlos and from Pablo. But let the would-be cat enthusiast be aware that this feline love and loyalty is only won with continuous effort and is not to be achieved lightly or just because you give a cat a home.

I have described the process of ultimate bonding with Carlos as an example. I find it a matter of no wonder that the Ancient Egyptians worshipped cats: for them cats had a divine right and it was only what the cats richly deserved. I must admit that I am smitten and cannot contemplate life without the love and companionship of our cats.

As one pedigree cat breeder once remarked to me when I pointed out that there are many people who actively dislike and even hate cats she said: 'Those people can never have known a Maine Coon.'

Soon Carlos would have been with us for three months. That meant that he was approaching six months old and it was time for him to be neutered. Since it was approaching Christmas I thought it best to get it over with before the holidays. I felt it advisable with our past record not to go to the vets we previously used, where Carlos and I had most certainly upset the management. There was another vet's surgery and I took Carlos there to be neutered and have an identity chip inserted under his skin in case he was ever lost or stolen.

I was told to collect him after three hours and as usual I spent the waiting time in a state of nervous tension. This state of mind was in no way diminished when I arrived at the surgery to be told that a vet wished to speak to me. Once I was ushered into her office I was relieved to be told that Carlos was fine but that in order to anaesthetize him it had required more of the chemical than usual. Therefore, he was still rather groggy and would need to be kept warm and offered plenty of water until he recovered.

I thanked her and was shown to a room where a dozy-eyed Carlos seemed as much relieved to see me as I was to see him. He slept flat-out all the way home and when laid comfortably by the fire with a bowl of water nearby he perked up momentarily, though sleep swiftly overcame him again.

Later, when Pablo came in for dinner, the noise awoke Carlos and he tried in vain to get up and go to the kitchen to see Pablo and possibly eat a few biscuits, but his back legs wouldn't work. The sight of him in this state made Catherine most distressed and she lay beside him on the floor stroking and talking to him all the while. I sought to reassure her by saying that 'wound up for action' was Carlos' normal state, which is why he behaves in such a hyperactive way, but tonight, because he was so heavily drugged, he was completely relaxed. It seemed odd to us because we had never seen him like this before.

'I thought you had managed to change all that,' Catherine said.

'I cannot change what God put there,' I commented. 'But

now that Carlos is so attached to me I can control him more easily and that is all I can do because he will always be highly strung, which is why the vet must have had to give him a real "Mickey Finn" to knock him out. He'll be his old self in no time.'

When we were satisfied that he was resting peacefully we left him stretched out in front of the fire and retired to bed. I was exhausted; we all were: it had been quite a day.

Sure enough, in the morning all was well and after a good night's sleep Carlos had made a full recovery. After a hearty breakfast of biscuits (he refused to eat cat meat), he appeared ever ready to resume living life to the full. A domestic incident then occurred that just showed how fully recovered he was from the anaesthetic and back to his hyperactive self.

It took place in the conservatory when Catherine and I were having a mid-morning coffee break. Carlos was staring out of the glass door leading into the garden when, because some of his fine hairs had got up my nose, I sneezed violently. Carlos, taken aback by the sudden explosive noise, leapt or, I should say, levitated on all fours to a height of at least six inches: he looked like a Harrier Jump Jet doing an aerial take-off. That was how highly strung our silver cat was all the time. Needless to say, the sight of his reaction made us both roar with laughter, especially since Carlos, now grounded again on all fours, turned to look at me in amazement. He couldn't work out why I had made such a loud noise.

Now that he had been neutered it was time to liberate him

from, as it were, domestic house arrest and give him his freedom to wander at will. I can't say how many times I have regretted this decision which effectively sealed his fate but at the time it seemed the right thing to do and it was evident that Carlos was enthused with joy the moment I opened the door and let him go. He bounded out into the garden and then whimsically turned and waited for me to join him. 'Go on, you're free now!' I called to him.

Suddenly from further up the garden Pablo appeared with a small rabbit in his mouth. As soon as Carlos spotted him he raced up the grass to greet him and share in the spoils. Pablo, much startled at the sight of Carlos, dropped the rabbit in surprise. Instantly, Carlos rushed to pick it up but not being big enough as yet he couldn't lift it clear of the ground and, in a pathetically funny attempt to cope, began to drag the dead creature down the path towards me. The rabbit became entangled in his legs and Carlos tripped and proceeded to fall over. Pablo meanwhile stared at this performance in disbelief.

This farcical situation was ended when I retrieved the rabbit carcass from a confused Carlos and disposed of it out of sight of the two cats. Pablo, deprived of his kill, disappeared over the garden fence post haste, followed by Carlos, who considered this to be a wise move in the circumstances.

Meanwhile I was left in a state of hiatus wondering if I would ever see him again. But true to form they both reappeared some hours later for dinner, rest and recreation. Soon Pablo and Carlos were to be found lying side by side in front of the sitting room fire in a seemingly comatose state, as only cats can achieve at a moment's notice. Catherine and I looked at each other and sighed with contentment that peace at last reigned in Owl Cottage. But for how long?

It was a few days before Christmas Eve and the business of decorating the tree and hanging tinsel, coloured lights and red-berried holly from the garden was in full swing at Owl Cottage. Once the cottage was seasonally decorated the cooking preparations commenced with turkey, vegetables and various sweatmeats and desserts being assembled and made ready. To me there is an excitement about Yuletide which no other time of the year quite manages to achieve. Most probably that is to do with feelings of vintage childhood nostalgia.

On the Monday of Christmas week there had been flurries of snow all day and hopes were running high for a White Christmas. When evening came the air temperature dropped sharply and snow began to fall in earnest. Before long the topmost branches of the fir trees in the garden developed a frosty mantel, followed by rooftops covered in thick blankets of white and then the garden at ground level disappeared under thick, powdery snow.

It was on this night as I watched the snow falling that Carlos set off on a new escapade, although I must say it progressively developed into something of a nightmare, rather than an adventure, for the two of us.

Pablo came into the cottage at the appointed time, consumed

his dinner and then hurried off, no doubt on a hunting spree, since the rabbit population was at the climax of its breeding cycle and there would be some tiny newborn bunnies to be dug out from burrows to provide tasty after-dinner morsels. Of Carlos there was no sign. This was unusual because the one thing that the silver cat craved more than excitement was his supper of special cat biscuits containing high energy and vitamin nutrition.

Several visits to the garden failed to elicit a response from Carlos despite loud whistling and calling. In common with other caring cat owners, whenever a beloved pet fails to appear as expected it rapidly develops into a cause for worry. And so it was with me. I could not rest until I knew what had happened to delay him and, naturally, I began to fear the worst.

An hour later and still there was no sign of him. Really alarmed at this point I set out with torch and stick in hand to look for him. I searched first the roads in the near vicinity, which were the most dangerous areas for any animal but especially cats. Thankfully I found no squashed corpses on the tarmac.

Returning home cold, wet and covered in snow after a fruitless search of hedgerows and ditches, not to mention a foray into the eerie darkness of adjacent woodland, I was tired. But after a reviving cup of tea laced with brandy and moral support from Catherine, I was ready to resume searching since I couldn't relax until I knew what had happened to Silver Boy.

Outside Owl Cottage the wind had whipped the lying snow

into icy flurries that stung my face and hands. By midnight I was tired of trudging around snowy pathways and neighbours' driveways and returned to the cosiness of the cottage when just on the edge of the wind I thought I caught the sound of a high-pitched wail coming from overhead. There it was again. A piercing note of sheer desperation. I knew it had to be Carlos.

At first I could not locate the sound. Thinking it might have come from the top of one of the tall trees that line the roadside, I flashed my torch to sweep across the bare upper branches but nothing registered in the light beams. Then a slight distance away a movement caught the periphery of my eye. Walking nearer and shining my torch upwards in the direction of the movement I saw the bright green reflection of a cat's eyes. And there he was, marooned on the ledge of my next-door neighbour's tall chimney stack. It was Carlos sure enough. He sounded petrified. Shining my light directly on him I could see that he was dodging around the base of the chimneys pots in agitated movements, slipping slightly on the snow as he lost his grip. It was as if he wanted to climb down but each time he approached the edge he lost his nerve and retreated, howling. He needed help. He cut a forlorn, increasingly snow-covered figure, tiny against the dark sky.

I got as close as I could to him from my position at ground level. Moving my torch around I shone it directly on to the roof tiles below Carlos and called his name again and again in the hope of giving him reassurance by my presence so that he could feel sufficiently confident to clamber down and come to me. No

matter how I urged him by calling out endearments and inducements he remained confined to the ledge. The only reply to my
summons was another series of louder whines and wails.

At first I was at a loss to understand his reluctance simply to
jump down and come to me. Then I recalled Catherine, who I
had noticed that Carlos, unusually for a cat, did not appear to
be adept at balancing on narrow ledges, and while sitting in the
garden we had been amused at his clumsy manoeuvres when
climbing in the trees. He could climb up well enough: it was
getting down that posed a problem. In comparison to Pablo he
had a lot to learn because the older cat was gifted with superb
agility.

Looking up at Carlos now, shuffling anxiously in the snow
around the chimney pots, it was clear that having jumped up on
to the chimney stack he was too scared to come down. So began
a number of ploys to rescue him. First I got the stepladder from
the garage and heaved my by no means agile body on to the
lower roof of my neighbour's house. Having gained a foothold
on the now freezing snow I crawled my way up into a lead-
covered gutter that led straight to the base of the chimney
where Carlos was now reduced to sitting and uttering plaintive
whimpers of distress. Unfortunately, the gutter was so slippery
that my attempts to advance higher resulted in an
unceremonious slide off the roof and, failing to grab the
stepladder, I was dumped down into the snow. By this time
Catherine had come out of Owl Cottage, just in time to see me
fall. She rushed over to help me up, frightened that I had hurt

myself badly. I hadn't but I was sure that I would feel bruised and sore the next morning. She advised me that it was now well after midnight and if the neighbours heard me thumping about they could well send for the police and I would be arrested.

Carlos obviously wanted me to come and get him but attempts to lure him off the chimney had failed completely and now my slide down the lower roof sealed his fate. I was beginning to feel very cold as the temperature continued to fall.

Just then Pablo, alerted no doubt by the goings-on, appeared on the roof from which I had fallen. My hopes of Pablo helping Carlos to find a way down grew. But that did not work either. Whether it was because of the cold or fear or maybe a combination of both, Carlos seemed almost unable to move. Completely exhausted by the whole escapade I could not think of what to do next. Catherine suggested we should go indoors before we caught pneumonia. She was right. Carlos would have to find his own way down.

I decided that if he wasn't down by the morning I would have to marshal help to rescue him but now bed and hopefully sleep beckoned, even though I hated the thought of abandoning him to the freezing cold weather outside.

Neither of us slept well that night. I tossed and turned in between short snoozes all night long. At last, when the illuminated dial of the bedside clock showed 6 a.m., I could no longer stay in bed and worry drove me to get up. Easing myself gently out of bed in the darkness so as not to disturb Catherine, whom I suspected was also half-awake because she was equally concerned for Carlos, I made my way quietly downstairs and had a reviving mug of tea. Not yet prepared to look outside I did not draw back the curtains covering the patio door adjacent to the kitchen, which is normally where both boys wait for us each morning after they have been out on their overnight prowls. But as I sat struggling with the dilemma of how to rescue Carlos there came a thumping and padding of paws against the door. That would be Pablo, I reckoned, back from his nightly excursions and no doubt with his superior feline senses he had detected that somebody was already up at this early hour.

'So why isn't the door open and breakfast served?' I guessed he'd be thinking. 'Well never let it be said that I am anything but a willing slave to the needs and wants of my cats,' I said to myself as I drew back the curtains. It was still dark outside and just as I opened the door, to my astonishment, a small grey and silver body shot inside, almost bowling me over in the process. It was Carlos, cold and hungry but otherwise unharmed. Following him at a leisurely saunter was a rather smug-looking Pablo, whose facial expression and body language suggested that he might well have had something to do with Carlos making a safe descent from the chimney. I hugged them both, Carlos especially. My feelings went into freefall and I could rejoice at all the good things in life once more. Just then Catherine appeared and together we were able to celebrate Carlos' safe return over breakfast.

Such are the problems to be expected when living with cats. Despite this episode and the snow, and in some respects perhaps because of it, we all had an especially happy Christmas at Owl Cottage. As ever, the cottage looked a picture with our Christmas cards, decorations and the Christmas tree itself, as well as the lights and candles, all enhanced by our newly acquired wood-burning stove.

The broader issue of training Carlos to become better disciplined was of necessity addressed by me every day and it soon reached the stage where I was able to say that it was working. I recalled a remark made to me by a horse wrangler I met when I was on a working holiday on a ranch in British Columbia in Western Canada: 'If you really want to tame a horse and teach it to like and respect you then don't set out to break its spirit. Talk softly to it. Spend time brushing it down whilst praising it for the horse you want it to be. Never use the whip. Then you'll have a friend and a helpmate for the rest of its life.'

It became clear in my mind that the same tactics could be applied equally to cats and indeed any animal to which you wished to relate. And by and large these were the tactics I had successfully used with my cats, not least Carlos who was now eight months old and growing fast, although he would never be as big a cat as Pablo.

By this time Carlos accompanied me in the car without demur and walked on the lead without complaint. But I feel I cannot overstate enough that the kind of interaction evident between Carlos and me, which resulted in these behavioural changes, was a two-way process. As the bonding grew firmer between us I became as closely attached to him as he was to me. A sort of emotional fine-tuning into what the other is feeling and experiencing occurs. I became aware that such an affinity was certainly beginning to grow between myself and Carlos just as it had happened in the past, only more so, with Toby Jug. In his case I only needed to look at him and I could weigh up his mood state. And it became obvious that when we were together Toby could respond to whatever I was feeling. If I was in a thoughtful mood he would join me on my knee and we would peruse the world together. If I happened to be low in spirit or upset he would do his best to console me by rubbing himself against me and licking my hand or neck and purring his song of love.

With Carlos the same sort of attachment was beginning to develop. One instance I can recall vividly. At the time it occurred it both thrilled and surprised me. I had noticed that Carlos, like kittens everywhere, liked to play with small objects, a rolled up piece of paper, a ball of some sort or just his own tail. But the difference with Carlos was that he would carry the object around in his mouth until he found a place to hide it. The next time I saw him do this I called him to me, rolled up a piece of paper and scrunched it into a ball. I showed it to him and he tried to take it from my hand but instead of giving it to him I threw it across the room. He stared at me in puzzlement and then charged after it, grabbed it in his mouth and disappeared into the hallway, obviously to hide it away. Later he came back into the room and sat by me.

'Why didn't you bring the paper ball back to me and then we could play a game?' He looked up at me with those large intelligent eyes and wandered off to sit near the fire. I returned to reading my book and thought no more of it.

Sometime later when Catherine came into the room, ever the tidy maid, she asked, 'What's that piece of paper doing down by your chair?' I glanced at the floor and there was the paper ball I had thrown for Carlos. He must have gone for it while I was reading and placed it near my shoe. But why? Surely he could not have understood my words. Had he read my mind? I told Catherine what had happened and she said, 'Why not try him again?' So I did. Picking up the paper I scrunched it in my hand until I attracted his attention and then I threw it to a far corner of the room. Without hesitation he galloped after it, took it in his mouth and raced back to me, dropped the paper ball at my feet and then stared up at me in anticipation of yet more fun. I stroked and patted him and told him how marvellous he was.

'Could be a coincidence, I suppose,' said my wife, mindful of me jumping to hasty conclusions. But after several repeat performances we became convinced that Carlos, incredulous as it seems, had understood what I wanted him to do. Highly elated that my cat was something of a genius I telephoned Jane, the breeder, to tell her about the incident, only to be somewhat deflated by her response. 'Oh there's nothing unusual about that with a Maine Coon cat. Many of my cats have retrieved and I've been constantly surprised at how quickly they pick up my thoughts,' she said in a matter-of-fact manner. Then she gave me a boost by adding: 'You need to remember that I am with my mother cats and their litters at the moments of their birth and for three months after that so they relate to me intimately, but you must have worked very hard with your kitten to achieve that quality of rapport.' I thanked her and rang off. Going back into the sitting room I picked up Carlos, hugged him and told him what a wonderful cat he was and how I loved him to bits. It had been hard work with him but now we were reaping the rewards.

After the several crises we had faced with Carlos, life at Owl Cottage at last began to resume its normal pattern. Together with our cats we were looking forward to the coming of spring. Each of the seasons has a distinctive charm but for me it is only springtime that has an appeal which is totally alluring. Here in Northumberland the snowdrops and crocuses usually come later than in the rest of the country but they are no less welcome. When I see the first daffodils flowering in the garden my spirit soars. The sight of those huge golden heads is uplifting, as is the appearance everywhere that I look of life renewing itself before my very eyes.

There is no green as vibrant and brilliant as the first leaves on our trees and remarkably each genus of tree seems to have its own unique shade of green. I so look forward to that time. When in tranquil moments, usually with a cat or two by my side, my mind becomes awash with the sheer beauty and inspiration of spring. I know that I am not the only one to be so stimulated because all around me the music of songbirds is heralding a time of rebirth. Above all, I am always relieved at the going of winter but I know that we will have to endure the snow and ice of wintry landscapes yet again because the exuberance of spring and summer needs some respite before we can be entranced by it once more.

And so I waited and prepared for the full onset of spring which was still some months away; it was time to turn my attention to the plants I grow each year in the greenhouse. My specialities are tomatoes and cucumbers, which I grow from seed obtained from far-flung countries of the world. This year I had an apprentice who would undoubtedly scrutinize my every move: his name was Carlos. Meanwhile, he liked to lie alongside my seed catalogues which were spread about on the table. Ever watchful, his attention followed whatever I did. Occasionally he would extend a paw and flick one of my pens towards him which he would then start to chew. If I got up to fetch something from the garage, for instance, Carlos would simultaneously rise, often from a state of apparent deep sleep, to follow me. It is what psychologists call 'pairing' or as my American friends put it, simply 'being buddies and pals'. I find it most endearing. You are never alone with a cat.

Since we got our boys I have found out that Maine Coons owe their existence to the actions of Marie Antoinette, the fateful Queen of France in the late eighteenth century. A virtual prisoner of royal protocol since her birth, she found solace and comfort in her pets and was especially fond of cats. She interbred some newly acquired Norwegian Forest cats, who were popular as rat-catchers aboard ships, with her long-haired pedigree lap-cats. Over several generations of breeding, a different type of cat emerged. These large and extremely handsome cats were considered to be exceptional because of their intelligence and affability. When the revolutionaries began to attack the French aristocracy, the Queen dispatched her beloved cats en masse by ship to the Americas, fully intending to follow herself. However, on her journey to the port, travelling in a coach bearing the royal insignia, she was stopped, taken captive, put on trial and ultimately guillotined. Her cats, meanwhile, survived and became most popular in that part of America called Maine on the east coast.

Since these cats shared a likeness both in appearance and habits with raccoons, the local populace mistakenly believed that they were hybrids produced by interbreeding the cats with raccoons, which is biologically impossible; hence they became known as Maine Coons even though they are most specifically of the cat species. Maine Coon cats are registered as a separate pure-bred pedigree cat nowadays and are extremely popular throughout the world.

In this period of relative calm at Owl Cottage I began to think that life with our two Maine Coons might endure in tranquil and uneventful mode for the foreseeable future. Then the unexpected happened. Pablo did not return from his Friday night out 'on the tiles'. Catherine and I had composed for our own amusement a fantasy storyline to describe what our magnificent cat did when he took off on his all-night prowls. My favourite idea was that he was on 'The Trail of the Lonesome Pine', culled from a song in one of the Laurel and Hardy films, because I knew that he ranged far and wide on his hunting excursions.

We had never been really worried about Pablo because he was so careful and cautious by nature, not at all excitable and impulsive like Carlos. He could be depended upon to have his jaunt every night and turn up tired and hungry each morning as regular as clockwork. That is, until one morning, which we never believed would come, when he wasn't there and did not appear all day. Later that morning I set out on that most feared duty of pet owners: the search for the body, dead or alive. Several hours later, I had no news for Catherine, who had been keeping watch for him at Owl Cottage. Of Pablo I had found no sign.

The next morning brought renewed hopes but there was no welcome furry presence at the patio door when we drew back the curtains. There was no sign of him for the rest of the day either or for the following two days. No sign or sight of him anywhere.

If you let cats roam free there is always the chance that you will lose them, victim to one or another of the myriad dangers out in the world. You take a real risk. Such were the thoughts going through my mind as it moved into hyperdrive and I began to imagine all kinds of disaster scenarios. Perhaps he was caught in a snare or trap like Toby Jug's mother had been the night I rescued her. There were still farmers and poachers in the area who laid traps. Perhaps he had been shot by a feckless poacher who hunted at night with lantern and shotgun and who would shoot any small animal that moved within range. Was he lying somewhere, wounded or dead? Reasoning it through, I determined to employ an age-old country remedy of using an animal to find an animal. I did not have a dog which I could use to track Pablo but I could hire the next best thing, a horse. Horses have extraordinary senses, as I had learned during my time on the trail in Western Canada. A horse is fundamentally a creature attuned to everything in the natural environment. My human perceptions could miss detecting an animal in distress but a horse would not. A horse would alert me to a suffering creature in the vicinity. And so I headed to a nearby farm where there was a riding school.

Green Meadows Riding School was managed by a pleasant lady named Molly who had that robust outdoor look, brimming with health. She listened sympathetically to my request to hire one of her horses for an unaccompanied ride around the local fields and woods. I didn't mention Pablo but simply explained that I had once kept a horse and now that I was retired I wished to take up riding again. I said I didn't need instruction and preferred to ride alone. She looked rather dubious at this and after some moments of deliberation she declared that I would need to demonstrate that I could ride safely in the indoor training ring. I had to agree. After all, it was only fair since I was a stranger to her.

I accompanied her to the stable area where she introduced me to a young mare called Starlight, suggesting that she might be suitable as a possible mount. However, the vibes coming from the horse were negative as far as I was concerned. For one thing she jerked her head about a lot, rolled her eyes and stamped a hoof as if she was anxious to be out and off. I imagined that Starlight would be something of a handful, more suitable to strong, older teenage girls than me. So I asked if there were any other mounts available. She pondered a moment and then she said she had a gelding called Rio who was a quiet, biddable ride and liked an easy life. 'I couldn't have put it better myself,' I said. Rio occupied a corner stall and looked out at me with mild liquid eyes and a steady gaze. I fondled his head and stroked his side and he stood without moving, enjoying the attention. I turned to Molly and indicated that I would try him.

Ten minutes later I was sitting astride Rio, wearing an infernal contraption called a safety helmet. I really did feel ridiculous but Molly insisted that it was regulation headwear, whilst staring disapprovingly at my past-their-best trainers and worn jeans. She also stressed the necessity of me donning a padded vest to protect my torso. If these safety measures had been in force when I first learned to ride then I doubt whether I would have ever started. I felt as if I were a jockey preparing to ride in the Grand National horse race. Struggling to hide my irritation I gave Rio a gentle heel and he lumbered into a jerky trot which I smoothed out by rising to the trot, although I much prefer the American western style of lengthening the stirrups and sitting solidly in the saddle. I feared Milady would not approve.

I circled the track a couple of times in this way and then pressed my knees slightly to spur Rio into a comfortable rocking horse canter. I reined him back and stroked and patted him a lot, all the while talking softly to him. Then I turned him this way and that, backing him up as if I were manoeuvring to open a gate, after which I rode him around again at a fast trot. I pulled up, looked over at Molly and asked if I'd passed.

'Well it's hardly "Horse of the Year Show" standard but I can see that you know how to handle a horse.' We then agreed terms and I paid her £80 for three hours. The price included the hire of the helmet, vest and also insurance. I considered it reasonable, especially if Rio helped me to find Pablo.

I mounted in the yard and urged Rio out on to the road, which I quickly crossed, and made my way along a farm track until I was well out of sight of the stables. Then I halted and, taking a green bin-bag from my pocket (I'd brought several with me in case I found Pablo's body), I placed the helmet and vest inside and hid the bag behind a hedge whilst holding firmly on to Rio in case he decided to head back home. Then, to Rio's growing interest, I took an apple from my pocket and cutting it in half I gave a section to him. He began to pay full attention to me now. I needed an alert horse under me and to achieve this I needed to have a degree of rapport with the animal.

Mounted again, with the breeze blowing in my face and ruffling my hair, I felt at home once more on horseback. I was now able to focus on the purpose of the ride as Rio trotted along the margins of the dormant fields. There was no sign of Pablo anywhere. No sounds of distress registered with either man or horse in response to my urgent whistles and calls. I rode by endless ditches and hedgerows, through scrub and deep copses, and picked my way through scattered and variegated patches of woodland.

I stopped and greeted two farmhands driving tractors over newly ploughed fields but they had seen nothing of a large brown cat. However, they did mention, just to make me feel worse, that they had seen a fox with cubs near the river. I dismounted and let my horse drink from a brook near the Coquet and considered my options.

I had been riding for two hours and was beginning to tire. I also felt that Rio had just about had enough. Besides that, my knees were in severe torment at the unaccustomed riding exercise and I felt it was time to call it a day. I fed Rio the rest of the apple and he looked at me with such big sorrowful eyes that I had to smile as I stroked him, although I felt far from happy.

As a last resort I led Rio up to the crest of a hill overlooking the river and using my small powerful binoculars I scanned the fields and the sky for any sight of buzzards, ravens or carrion crows which might be circling around a trapped or dying animal. There was nothing to be seen, the sky was empty of life and despite my thick sweater I was beginning to feel chilled now that the late February sun had clouded over. Remounting, I turned Rio for home and for the first time felt some exuberance in his fast trot and short canters. This horse liked an easy life and he had probably covered more ground that afternoon than he normally did in a week but he had done well for me. Also riding-school horses ordinarily ride out in a bunch and he had most likely missed the company of the others. Retrieving the bag in which I'd hidden the safety gear I led Rio on foot to ease my back and knees and handed him over to a waiting stable girl.

Returning home I could only wearily shake my head at Catherine's questioning looks as I headed for the bathroom and a welcome hot bath.

Lying awake in bed that night I tried to think of what else I could do to find Pablo. If he was dead then the least I could do was find his body and bring him home. But where could he be? It had been four days since we had last seen him. I was acting on the good old British Army strategy that there is always something more that you can do. After a while a memory from the past crept into my head of a friend called Duncan with whom I had, over a glass or two of wine, shared many discussions on such topics as folklore and psychology. As I recall, Duncan had either been related to gypsies, now called travellers, at a settlement near Yetholm in Northumberland, or had even spent some of his formative years in their company. He related to me many tales of gypsy power spells and magic practices which could be used to help with problems of everyday living, although we tended to agree that so-called 'magic' was an unconscious function of the human mind set on achieving something or other. Gypsy 'spells' involved ways of focusing mental powers in order to create good outcomes. I suppose this could be described as a means of praying or, as research in areas of phenomenological psychology states: if you can visualize something strongly enough then you can actualize it for real. That is, you can make things happen through the power of the mind.

As my thoughts meandered along these lines I suddenly realized that my brain was trying to figure out a solution to Pablo's disappearance. I recalled Duncan telling me that when someone went missing the gypsy method of guiding them home was to inscribe the person's name on a white candle and light it in a window to call the lost one back. It was a way of focusing the feelings to summon the lost one back home. Then my thoughts made another connection to a story by Charles Dickens in which a candle was left burning each night to lead 'Little Dorrit' home.

Excited now that I had something else to try I hurried downstairs. In our candle box I found a medium-sized white candle on which I wrote the name Pablo in red ink. This I placed in an antique candle holder that had once belonged to my grandmother and which we always used at Christmas. Lighting the candle with a hand that shook with all the nervous energy of worrying about him, I whispered a prayer that the light from this candle would bring Pablo home safe and sound. I carried the candle upstairs and placed it on the uncurtained hall window facing out over the garden and fields beyond.

I replaced the candle at regular intervals and kept it burning day and night. The next night as I mounted a vigil by the open window, a curious silver cat joined me and kept watch with me each night afterwards. I realized that it gave me something to do which gave me hope, but gradually my hopes for the return of our lovely big brown boy were fading as the amount of time that had elapsed since his disappearance increased.

On Friday it would be a week since he had last been with us. If he were alive but trapped somewhere without food and water then his chances of survival were minimal. Catherine and I both became convinced that we would never see him again and with that realization melancholia set in. We did not talk much. We each moved quietly about our business of the day with heavy hearts, as if we had only just grasped how much the presence of Pablo meant to us. Without closure of some sort we could not begin to put our memories to rest.

Late on Friday evening Catherine and I sat talking in the conservatory. I could tell that she had shed a few tears over Pablo but I did not remark on it because I also felt devastated. She and I agreed that it was not realistic for either of us to go on hoping for his return. We knew that everything that we could do to find him had been done. We commented that since he had an identity chip he could easily have been identified if he had been found then. But a large cat like Pablo could range over great distances and we had to accept he might never be found. Anything might have happened to him. We had given him his freedom which he seemed to enjoy and this was the price we had to be prepared to pay for that.

Many people in our little hamlet and the extended village of Felton called to sympathize with us once they heard about our loss. Catherine had told the girls at the hairdressers and I had put a notice in the post office window. In our small rural community, where most people know each other, there prevails a sense of communal concern for neighbours when any kind of problem or tragedy happens. The Village Coffee Shop is more than just a cafe as it tends to be a meeting place for local folk where news is dispensed via the grapevine and it was my hope that eventually someone would find out what had happened to Pablo.

As Catherine and I sat talking we began to share some of our personal memories of Pablo. She recalled how on some mornings after he had eaten his breakfast he would insist on coming to lie in her lap and refuse to budge until he had his expected half-an-hour stroke and cuddle.

For my part, and I had not told her this before, I remembered how if he was in the mood he would greet me by jumping on the table or windowsill and, rising up, he would place his massive paws on my shoulders and rub his face against mine, especially the sides of my head. Of course, I loved this display of affection. And cringing somewhat to disclose such a private moment to another person, I recalled my use of a silly affectionate pet name for him: I called him my 'Big Teddy Bear'. Also I sometimes would pick him up two-handed, with his front paws in my left hand and his back legs in my right hand, swing him over my head and wrap him around my neck like a scarf; he loved it and would purr away loudly to let me know how pleased he was.

And so we talked away our sorrows as the evening progressed until at last we felt a little better and decided to call it a day. As I headed up to bed I took a last look out the window where the candle was still burning as a testimony to our love for our missing Maine Coon. At midnight it would be three days since I had lit the first candle. With a jolt I remembered Duncan's words: 'In gypsy lore the candle will work within three days or not at all.' Oh well, I thought, at least I tried everything.

Just then Carlos joined me noisily on the window sill. He put his face close to the glass window and cried excitedly. 'I don't think so, Carlos,' I said and opened the window so that we could both look out. 'See,' I said to him, 'there's nothing there. Pablo will not be coming home but he'll always be with us won't he?' Just as I uttered the words a whiff of air blew out the candle. 'There you are! That's an end to it.' And I closed the window. Then I opened the back door for him to saunter forth.

We slept later than usual and so it was nearly 9 a.m. before I ushered Carlos in from the garden to feed him. After his breakfast he liked to retire to the conservatory to watch the birds and the garden, and to indulge in a morning nap after the exertions of prowling throughout the night. I was feeling desperately low.

Later that morning I took my third cup of coffee into the study to do some reading as I didn't feel up to writing. Catherine was meanwhile working on the computer to prepare some items for the forthcoming Parish Council Meeting for which she was Clerk. She looked unhappy. However, outwardly it appeared that all was calm within Owl Cottage. The bright early morning sun was melting last night's harsh white frost which covered the entire garden.

Suddenly, there came a tremendous crash and sound of breaking glass. Catherine beat me to the scene of the disaster and I heard her exclamations of dismay. I bet it's Carlos, I thought. Surprisingly, my wife's cries changed to ones of jubilation. 'Denis,' she shouted. 'Come quickly and see. Your "Big Teddy Bear" is back! He's here now.' I literally could not believe my ears. With my heart thumping as if it would jump out of my chest I walked disbelievingly into the conservatory to see my wife on her knees, hugging a ragged looking Pablo.

'Well I never, how on earth . . .' I began. 'Pablo!' I shouted and then the feelings aroused were beyond words. The two of us simply petted and stroked him until we had the sense to appreciate that he must need water desperately and some food. But Pablo did not seem to mind and obviously enjoyed the attention he was getting more than anything else.

He did drink thirstily when we offered him water but ate only sparingly. What he seemed to need most of all was to be with us. After the initial petting session we examined him thoroughly and concluded that he had not been living outside. His fur was too smooth and dry and the pads of his paws, especially the claws, showed no sign of wear and tear. I was mystified as to where he could have been.

We wondered if someone had kept him prisoner, but then quickly dismissed that explanation since Pablo did not take to strangers easily and would become fierce if coerced in any way. Eventually, we assumed that he must have wandered into an open garage or outhouse and became captive when the owners locked up and went off for a week; this was probably the most likely explanation. It was highly unlikely that we would ever know for sure where he had been. He must have had access to water, possibly condensation on a window or steel door. It was all a puzzle to us.

We spent most of that day stroking and talking to him. For his part he simply lay there, enjoying the loving care and attention we lavished upon him. Relief was palpable in us all. We were both absolutely delighted and Carlos too seemed pleased. It was a momentous occasion, one to be recorded in the annals of Owl Cottage. Catherine opened a bottle of champagne she had been saving and I indulged a glass of single malt whiskey from a bottle I'd specially put aside. Pablo had come home and all was well with the world once more. Incidentally, the loud crash we had heard was caused by Carlos, (who else?), who must have spotted Pablo and became so excited that he ran amok and knocked over a vase of flowers. As we too had experienced a range of emotions over Pablo, we felt we could hardly blame our impulsive silver cat who still exhibited hyperactive tendencies from time to time. So what if the vase was broken and water spilled all over the hall carpet? (No cat is perfect.) Carlos welcomed Pablo back enthusiastically but insisted on having his fair share of the strokes being given out.

Later in the day I noticed that Catherine had already tidied away the antique candle holder and wiped up some spilt candle grease from the window sill. The sight of this started me thinking about what Duncan had told me regarding old-fashioned gypsy spells. Pablo had returned after the candle had burned for three days. Duncan had said everything works in threes, for example, three wishes, three coins in the well, cross your fingers and count to three, etc. I began to think that perhaps there was something in those old mystic lores that could not be easily explained away. I shook my head in disbelief as I reflected that there is much about this world that is beyond my understanding. But I was glad that Pablo was back, however it had happened.

Soon our minds were attuned to happier thoughts and feelings as spring finally arrived and all at once the garden and the trees began to show new life. It is at this time of the year that I most enjoy walking around the garden, usually in the early evening when the sunlight dims to a hazy glow and the earth shines in a golden half-light which the Scottish call the 'gloaming'. Then the colours of the flowers and the fruit blossom seem to radiate a lustre of their very own, as if they are giving back sunshine to illuminate the air. It is a special time for insects, too, among which only the bumble bees work with feverish haste in contrast to the fluttering butterflies, with wings softly hued, and flimsy damselflies iridescently shimmering as they hover above the waters of the bird bath. Such sights inspire the human heart and mind with poetic images and nourish the soul. In this vein of sheer delight, who would dare call my all-time favourite wild flower, the cowslip, a weed?

Reflections like this awaken nostalgic reminiscences of earlier times in my life when I'm afraid I became an inveterate truant from school. If on my journey to school a passing gleam of sunshine touched me then my longing for the dense greenery of fields and inviting riverbanks, the path through the woods and the excitement of the lake seen distant through the trees would turn me away to cavort as a free spirit among nature's bountiful offerings! To watch the nesting songbirds and to listen to their sweet whistling, to glimpse hares running wild across fields of waving grasses, to lie at ground level at the side of a pond and gaze in curious wonder at a stickleback in full mating regalia of black and red, weaving his nest of slime-green moss to attract a mate – this was the education for which I craved even though I knew that that a heavy punishment would be meted out both at home and at school when I was found out. I didn't care: it was worth it. That inevitable outcome never deterred me from my wild gambols with mother nature.

One morning as Catherine and I ate breakfast the boys, as we nearly always referred to Pablo and Carlos now, started making a real fuss at the conservatory window. When we looked out we saw what had bothered them: two frisky red squirrels were feeding from the peanuts we put out for the birds. I addressed the cats in human terms but they understood the tone of my voice alright: 'You've had your breakfast. Don't begrudge other animals a bite or two!'

While my cats show remarkable empathy towards us I'm afraid that does not extend to other species. And so, in spite of their insistent demands to be let out, I refused and watched in fascination the acrobatic antics of the squirrels who were hanging upside down, taking nuts and seeds from the bird-feeders. Both cats continued to make throaty growls, turning their backs to me in a huffed posture and declining to make eye contact for the rest of the morning.

But this was unusual; normally we are easy with each other, born out of the reciprocity I described earlier. The cats and I spend blissful hours together just watching the garden, the trees, the birds and the wildlife and I assume that they, like me, enjoy it. We stare out of the large windows of the conservatory, sometimes at a sky laced with orange and yellow woven against a backcloth of azure and indigo as the evening sun softens into lingering twilight. A faint breeze might stir the grass and bushes around the trunks of the trees, disturbing a male blackbird who screeches and tweaks his tail in a spasm of agitation before flying on to the top of the garage roof to deliver his evening serenade. Much later, the creeping darkness hides everything until a three-quarter moon lightens up the sky and intensifies the watching as the creatures of the night begin to emerge. Along the fringes of the far line of trees at the end of the garden and, in the patches of meadow, moonbeams call out hedgehogs, moles and field mice to move afoot in their everlastingly urgent search for food. A whole array of moths takes to the air with the inevitable consequence that the bats, lying in wait, indulge in a feeding frenzy.

For my two cats this heralds a call to action; it is a time for stalking and the thrill of the chase, though I am confident that they won't overdo a killing spree because they are too well fed. The chase will be solely for fun. As they disappear into the night I move to relax my cramped limbs and go in search of a cup of tea and possibly a sandwich.

As the months passed, Catherine and I decided that we were in need of a holiday and on impulse we decided to go to the Isle of Wight. We organized a stay at the Blue Lodge, a local cattery, for the boys and although we knew they would have only the very best of care and attention, it was nevertheless a traumatic experience for all of us to be separated.

When we were ready to depart, we put Pablo and Carlos into a large carrying box together and placed it on the back seat of the car. The cats became aware that they were being taken either to the vet's or to the cattery and, although Carlos is used to the car, he joined in the whining distress calls of Pablo, which sounded dreadful. We became upset but we gritted our teeth, turned up the radio and reasoned that since we rarely go away, the cats would just have to make the best of it.

We returned home to finish packing. The cottage felt so empty and strange without our felines that we were glad to leave. We drove south on the M1 on a bright sunny morning in

June. We reached our night stopover just outside Oxford in the early evening. After a brief rest and freshen-up we went to a well-known watering hole called the Trout. The lovely day turned into a delightful warm evening full of sunshine and bird song. The Trout was situated in a charming old-world setting. From the car park we crossed a quaint wooden bridge over the river to enter, via a rustic gate, the Trout's open-air dining space which was shaded by an ancient oak tree growing in the centre. We chose a table lodged against the trunk of the oak, where we had a clear view of the river and a variety of water fowl which seem uncommonly tame. The young waitress who served us was a student in her second year studying languages at one of the colleges of Oxford University and we had a pleasant conversation with her about her home in South America.

The meal was excellent and the wine superb but just as we were lingering over a final glass, enjoying the balmy late night air, we were jolted out of our reverie by a hideous scream from some animal or other. We looked around and saw that many of our fellow diners, who were obviously regulars, were simply nodding and smiling at each other as if there was nothing untoward about the noise.

I followed the direction of their glances and spied a whopping great bird on the roof which was instantly accompanied by another. They flapped and strutted around, and then we heard strident screams repeated several times. I realized that we were being treated to an encounter with peacocks. These majestic birds with their fabulous fantail plumage must be a speciality of the inn but not for the menu! I expect that they are a customized extra to attract visitors because they certainly add something unusual to the already impressive ambience of the Trout Public House.

All at once one of the peacocks began to clamber in an ungainly but effective fashion down the tree under which we were sitting and, by a series of wing flaps and teetering grabs at the lower branches, the creature arrived at the base of the tree adjacent to our table. Subjecting us both to a goggle-eyed stare, it felt safe enough to thrust its long neck forwards and, dipping a coloured beak into a bowl on our table, began to consume mouthfuls of brown sugar. To our amazement this continued for some time until a passing waiter intervened and chased the bird away, whereupon it flew to roost on the roof and commenced more screaming. Turning to us the waiter remarked by way of explanation that this peacock was addicted to sugar and chocolates and the staff were under instructions to prevent the bird indulging.

As we left the restaurant we were passed on the bridge by a cream-and-auburn-coloured cat who did not acknowledge my greeting and hurried on inside, no doubt for a feast of meaty leftovers. Later, as I went to bed, my thoughts as ever switched to a place in Northumberland where I believed two Maine Coon cats would be thinking of us and I hoped they would know that we were missing them, too.

The next day we drove through the New Forest and savoured the experience of watching a group of wild ponies grazing in picturesque settings of the time-honoured variety, which served to remind us what we had read about the culture and history of this unique place. I would have liked to linger and absorb the vibes of the forest but Catherine, who is much better than I am at keeping to a timetable, urged us to press on for the car ferry. My lasting image of the area is a view of hazy sunshine outlining the silhouettes of horses and trees in woodlands looking much as they must have done for hundreds of years. It was almost like a watercolour painting.

A couple of hours later we began to feel that we were really on holiday when in warm sunshine we boarded the car ferry for Yarmouth, Isle of Wight. Driving around the island during our week's stay gave us a lot of pleasure. A special favourite route was the scenic road along the east coast up to Osborne House and Cowes. But we also enjoyed walking along the coast towards the Needles and the famous Alum Bay, with its multi-coloured cliffs and sand. Our seven days passed quickly and after taking a final coffee at a fine old hotel in Yarmouth we were on our way north. I was glad to be going home; I was seriously missing our cats.

This time our stopover for the night afforded us the opportunity to visit a hostelry dating back to Tudor times called the Coach and Horses Inn which had oak beams and white plaster walls, and was full of old-world charm. As we sat in antique chairs at a table which must have been early Victorian I felt fully relaxed in spite of the muted noise from a World Cup football match on the television in the bar next door.

After a very good dinner we sat relishing the last of our wine and the cosy comfort of the lounge when I noticed the entrance of an exceptional dog. He was long in body with the rangy look of a hound, possibly a wolfhound with some of the lurcher about his slender, smooth-haired frame. I frequently find that now I am retired as a psychologist, which involved a heavy clinical commitment to people, I take immense pleasure in applying my psychology to the study of animals, whether they are birds, horses, dogs or, more especially, cats. This dog looked a promising subject. It glided into the room as unobtrusively as a breath of air and his demeanour oozed breeding and class. His master sauntered into the bar as easily and nonchalantly as his dog and casually took a seat, which appeared to be reserved for him. His dog was already lying beneath the appointed table as if he and his master belonged there by right.

Although there were no other dogs around, no one seemed to object to this dog's presence, which surprised me. This dog was really far too big to be in this low-ceilinged, modest-sized room with what we decided must be the regular Saturday night crowd. The dog's owner, a man in his late fifties, evidenced an air of nobility and privilege in common with his dog. He appeared to be perfectly at ease with the world and himself. In keeping with his aristocratic airs he had an aura of eccentricity about him, too, as witnessed by the trousers he was wearing which appeared garish in their design of black stars and spots on a white background. The fact that he had the confidence to wear them in a public place and to bring with him a huge hound indicated that he probably belonged to the local gentry and this assumption was born out by the deference the staff showed towards him.

But more than the man, it was his magnificent dog which arrested my attention. He lay on the floor half underneath his master's table and only his eyes moved to convey that he was alert to everything going on in the room. In a while he sensed that I was studying him and gave me a long scrutinizing stare and then, concluding that I was without menace, he resumed his watchful gaze over the room. To give a dog like him the exercise he needed to keep fit would, I believed, require someone with a horse prepared to ride several miles a day. He seemed to be in magnificent condition judging from his well-groomed, fine-haired coat of muted brown. I sensed that his owner, who never once had to speak to him but did occasionally caress his ears, thought the world of him. I enjoyed the evening for many reasons but the sight of that superb animal in such harmony with his master, who obviously treated him very well, made the experience complete.

We made our way back to our hotel by taxi through the grandeur of richly endowed countryside which was a pleasure to see and was rendered all the more pastoral by the silver moonlight. I reflected on the sharp contrast between this lush landscape through which we were travelling and the harsh wilderness of the moors and hills of Northumberland where we lived. It made me think of how fortunate we are to have large tracts of land consisting of such diverse features of rural terrain covered by multiple flora and inhabited by a wide variety of wildlife which inspires the spiritual as well as aesthetic appreciation that has been lyrically described as 'Forever England'.

As I lay awake in our hotel, which nestled in woodland near a lake and was a fair distance from the M1 motorway, I could hear through the partially open bedroom windows the soft hooting of owls and once or twice I thought I caught the sounds of foxes barking a communication to each other as they hunted rabbits in moonlit meadows. Such sounds are a source of solace to me whenever I hear them and I believe them to be healing for anyone with a stressed or troubled mind. Humans cannot afford to separate themselves from the natural life of our planet. It set me thinking of how our domesticated creatures can provide us with friendship, solace and succour and how helpful and supportive these relationships can be especially when we are troubled.

For example, I was told about a woman who lived not many miles from us in a fishing village who could often be seen walking around with an exotically coloured parrot on her shoulder. This large bird was, it would seem, so attached to her that he demanded to be taken along wherever she walked in the locality. One summer evening I was extremely surprised to see this same lady as she entered a fish and chip shop where I was waiting my turn. On her left shoulder was perched the parrot, which proceeded at intervals to address the queue and the assistants with remarks such as 'Turned out nice again' and

'Two fish suppers please with batter'. These utterances were accompanied by much bowing and bobbing. The fact that no one else seemed to find this unusual convinced me that this was a regular performance. It was clear that the lady herself was extremely proud of her pet and his prowess with language as she stroked and cosseted him in a most loving manner. That woman and her parrot clearly gave each other a great deal.

Perhaps the English, as the saying goes, are truly a nation of animal lovers, although some events would appear to contradict that opinion, including an incident that happened in the neighbouring village of Felton. It was so extraordinary that it made local, national and then international headlines. It began first as a rumour spread by a few avid gardeners who circulated their anecdotes at the bar of the Northumberland Arms, which stands just over from the old bridge at Felton.

The story was that a giant rabbit was raiding crops of vegetables from the village gardens and allotments. Jokes galore made the rounds about the Giant Beast of Felton which could strip a garden of all its produce in a single night. At first the jokers had their way and every one believed the stories to be an elaborate hoax until a local housewife of mature years, and not one given to practical jokes, reported seeing a huge rabbit thundering across her lawn in the early morning rain. Other sightings followed and the continuance of the raids on vegetable plots by the strange creature outstripped the jokers and moved one besieged allotment holder, sixty-three-year-old Jeff Smith, to attempt to mobilize support from the local community, including the Parish Council, to eradicate this nuisance. With this in mind two local gamekeepers were instructed to stalk and shoot the animal. Immediately, there arose a concerted outcry from many within the village, including myself, and when the news got out people from outside the village voiced their protests at this draconian measure.

One misty morning I spotted this great rabbit moving around the far end of our garden. He was indeed massive, far outweighing the local population of wild rabbits, and I guessed he was a pet rabbit that had either been abandoned or had made a break for freedom. I watched him serenely cropping some long grass growing near a pear tree and as I moved from my seating position in the conservatory he saw me and did not take fright, thus confirming my original view that he was a tame pet rabbit. In contrast to my response, my cats were really spooked and were literally climbing up the walls in shock horror. I watched him as he loped off and bade him good luck: he would need it.

Heated arguments both for and against killing the monster sustained the public attention until it was suddenly realized that the rabbit had simply disappeared. Then further rumours began to disseminate regarding the fate of the creature and soon conspiracy theories, most of which were fuelled by alcohol, started to orbit around the town.

About a month after the gossip about the rabbit subsided I met up with a young lad I had known previously as a waiter in the Northumberland Arms but who was now working in a supermarket in Alnwick. We got talking and I mentioned the mystery of the 'Felton Rabbit'. He drew me aside in a secretive manner and confided that his uncle told him that a group of allotment holders had lain in ambush for it one night, shot it dead, skinned and barbequed it, and fed the meat to their dogs. I never found out if this was true but if it was then the poor rabbit had failed to understand that human domination of the animal kingdom is absolute and, although his life was as important to him as anybody else's is to them, once he came into conflict with man's interests he had to die.

This tragic affair called to mind how scientific institutions abuse animals for their own research purposes and I remember learning that one highly esteemed director of an animal research unit had published a paper describing an experiment in which twenty cats had been deliberately blinded to advance knowledge about eyesight. During my own university studies for a bachelor of science degree, in which I had to attend laboratory sessions in the department of zoology, I was made aware that compassion for our mammalian brethren was non-existent in the cause of science. It happened that one day my assignment in the physiology laboratory was to create a diagram of the organs and innards of a rat. I began carefully to copy the relevant details from the physiology chart manuals I had to hand when a lab assistant handed me a typed note which instructed me to kill one of the pure-bred white lab rats, then dissect it and note down the spatial distribution of its organs. Just as I finished reading the instructions I was handed a box full of cotton-wool pads, a bottle of chloroform and a live white rat. I need to point out that the white rats bred for experiments bear little resemblance to the wild brown breed that inhabit our countryside or the disease-carrying black rats of the sewers. The creature that sat on my table had pure white fluffy fur and pink eyes. In appearance it looked as harmless as a kitten and I truly felt that I was in the presence of a healthy, sentient animal. As I stared at it in consternation it ambled across towards me and licked the back of my hand.

I said, 'Don't worry, I won't kill you,' and I stroked its head. Then I became aware of a figure standing off to my right. It was the professor in charge of the session.

'This is not Pet's Corner, O'Connor. Complete your assignment.'

'Sir,' I called out, because he was already moving away. 'Please, sir, I don't need to kill this creature because I already have a detailed anatomy chart of the rat right here, which I'm in the process of copying. Also, I'm a psychology student not a medic!'

If you have ever been in the presence of a human being who looked as if he would explode then you will recognize my experience that afternoon. In short I was told that if I refused to carry out this assignment then I could say goodbye to any chance of graduating. In a frame of mind akin to being encased in a block of ice I did what I was expected and vowed that I would never ever again wittingly cause the death of an innocent animal. When I left the session I fled to the lavatory area and vomited. That evening I could not face dinner and sat in the student bar sipping a pint of lager and reflecting on Wordsworth's words about what man has done to man. And no, I didn't sleep well that night; I kept seeing a little white rat staring at me accusingly for taking his life as if it meant nothing. The note which passed my assignment as satisfactory added a cryptic footnote which said: 'There is no place in science for sentiment!'

As these memories of bygone days and experiences ranged hurtfully through my mind on the final night of our holiday, I suddenly felt very sleepy and the next I knew it was morning. As we ate breakfast the central thought in both our minds was that today we were going home to our cats and we would be happily with them by nightfall.

After an arduous journey by motorway we were reunited with Pablo and Carlos. The reunion was not without strain for us since we were treated, despite our enthusiastic petting and stroking, with the bland indifference that only cats can muster when they feel huffed by the absence of their loved ones. On arriving home friendly relations were only resumed after we had fed them and made an excessively big fuss of them both. Eventually Carlos, who could no longer maintain his aloofness, jumped on my knee and began to tread my sweater whilst emitting melancholy cries intermingled with purrs, just to let me know that he had missed me terribly but he was desperate to know why it was that I had left him anyway. Meanwhile, Pablo deigned to stretch his massive form across Catherine's lap and, in between a series of baritone purrs, commenced to lick her hand and arm. After a while feelings of domestic harmony pervaded the room and all was once more well at Owl Cottage. But this slightly tense reception by our cats due to our absence reminded me how much they were emotionally dependent on our presence and our love. The problem for animals is that when we leave them they cannot be sure that we will come back until we actually do return, which causes them extreme emotional distress. Being aware of this affects me so intensely that I have often considered whether I should ever leave them again for whatever reason.

The next day after we returned from holiday I resumed my focus of attention on training Carlos but I was beginning to believe that he had changed over the past few months and was fast becoming a more agreeable cat, although I understood that his personality would always retain a wild streak. He increasingly liked to spend time at my side, whatever I was doing. If I was still in bed in the morning he would seek me out and join me on the bed, where I was treated to a fulsome show of affection. If he caught me still asleep I would receive licks on the forehead and cheeks until I surfaced, blinking to find his handsome little face peering at me, exuding love and affection. Then he would work his way under the duvet and poke his head a little way out, which was a signal that he wished to be stroked. He would lie there next to me emitting throbbing purrs of sheer happiness which, in turn, made me happy, too. Since further sleep was impossible I would give him a few more moments of attention and then get up, escorted by this attentive cat who would weave between my legs as I descended the stairs, often in danger of tripping over because of him. Once I had my morning cup of tea he would jump on my knee, snuggle cosily into my dressing gown and look at me as if to say: 'Where are we going today, then?'

The intense look in his bright green eyes made to chuckle at the gung-ho, lively attitude of this cat. He truly was a rare phenomenon among his kind and I couldn't quite believe that in the short time we had been together he was beginning to mean everything to me. Each day I looked forward to his antics, which at one time had worried me. We were really getting to know each other. Lately, I had been concerned because of his preference for dried food over the meat varieties. I finally resorted to cooking chicken for the cats, especially Carlos, and even went to the extent of cutting fine slivers of chicken breast to tempt him. Whilst he would chew a couple of pieces just to please me he preferred to eat dry biscuits, which meant of course that he needed to drink lots of water. It distressed me to see how desperately he needed water: even though there was always a clean bowl of water for the cats in the conservatory, Carlos felt the necessity to stand on the edge of the kitchen sink, imploring me to turn on the cold water tap, and then eagerly lean forward to drink directly from the streaming water. This behaviour resulted in him becoming soaked to the skin on the upper parts of his body, though he didn't seem to care.

In the literature about Maine Coon cats there is particular mention made of their fancy to take to the water and all my cats, including Toby, loved washing a morsel of meat in their drinking bowl. Each summer we wash our cats in a bucket of warm water and they seem to really enjoy this for the soothing affect on their skin. We always choose a hot day so that they can dry off quickly. An exceptional incident of this kind took place with Toby Jug when he was about three years old.

One morning I was taking a shower and to my surprise he walked under the shower curtain and settled himself at my feet. Anxious that soap wouldn't get into eyes and hurt him, I switched off the shower head, lifted him out and commenced to dry him immediately. However, he appeared to be totally un-concerned and I do believe that the wily cat had kept his eyes closed. He repeated this deed on several other occasions when the weather was hot and more especially if I was having a cool shower after a day's gardening. Whilst Carlos never took a shower with me, he did enjoy taking a run through the automatic revolving garden hose spray when I fixed it to the lawn on especially hot sunny days.

Just as I became resigned the fact that Carlos would only eat dry biscuits I discovered that he liked milk pudding. One evening after dinner I opened a tin of creamed tapioca as a dessert for myself, since Catherine was enduring a self-imposed dieting regime. Once Carlos spied me eating the pudding he began to pester me for a taste. Assuming that Catherine's attention was elsewhere I poured a small spoonful on to a paper

I took Carlos to the beach at Bamburgh Castle.

I raced for the car with Carlos to escape the storm.

We lit a candle in the window to call Pablo home.

Max, the red kitten, is comforted by his little twin brother.

napkin for him to sample. Then two things happened at the same time. First, Catherine spotted what I had done in defiance of her right and proper ruling that cats were not to be fed at the table and I was subjected to a harsh reprimand. Second, Carlos consumed, in rapid time, not only the spoonful but also the part of the napkin on which it had lain. This feat reminded me again of Toby Jug, who also loved puddings, only in his case it was baby-food tins of chocolate pudding.

From that time on tapioca became a preferred culinary delight for Carlos, though he refused rice pudding and wouldn't touch semolina. For him it was obviously a matter of taste. In case he would felt left out and became jealous through sibling rivalry, a portion of tapioca was offered to Pablo. He sniffed it derisively then walked away with an expression which in plain cat language said: 'You can't expect me to eat that muck. Don't you know I'm a meat-eating cat exclusively?'

From then on the dry biscuit meals for Carlos were supplemented at intervals with a small portion of tapioca milk pudding, which caused me to reflect on the lengths to which I would go to please and care for our cats. Indeed, in so many ways life makes us hostage to the ones we love no matter who and what they are.

The emergence of other traits of personality which distinguished Carlos from other cats was epitomized by little incidents that occurred daily. When taking together all the facets and quirks of his behaviour, including his hyperactive approach to life, there was little doubt that he was a remarkable cat and that we had in our home a champion of the feline variety.

Carlos loved to play. He needed no prompting to race around the garden after me as I towed a length of plastic wrapping cord across the grass, though he found it too easy to catch me and so would attempt to rouse Pablo in a game of chase. One calm and sunny evening in May, Catherine and I were relaxing in the garden when we witnessed Carlos approaching Pablo, who was lying in the grass thinking cat things and doing nothing in particular. Carlos assumed an exaggerated side-on pose and pranced towards Pablo, who simply stared at him as if he considered this behaviour idiotic. Frustrated beyond bearing with the big cat, Carlos resorted to aggression and swiped Pablo across the face before racing off. When Pablo, looking dumbfounded, still didn't respond, Carlos charged him and a rousing chase and fight ensued with both cats running to and fro, accompanied by some squealing from Carlos as the larger, heavier cat sought to teach him a lesson. Eventually, the two cats lay down in the grass exhausted. But this incident made me realize that the over-the-top enthusiasm of Carlos did not gel with Pablo's more matter-of-fact, sober approach to living. We discussed the situation as we saw it and the upshot was that I determined to phone Jane, the Maine Coon breeder, the following day to order a new kitten to give Carlos a playmate. If I could acquire another cat of similar temperament to Carlos, but not excessively so, then it might satisfy his need to play and lift the onus from Pablo.

'I hope you know what you're doing,' my wife said.

'Well, he needs a companion something like himself so I'll see if Jane has any more silver boys on the way.'

'I just hope another silver kitten won't be as crazy as Carlos,' Catherine said.

'Don't worry. There couldn't be another the same as he is!' said I hopefully.

The next day Jane told me over the phone that her silver female called Florence had been mated again with Oscar, the six-times champion cat who had a formidable reputation as a stud and, incidentally, was the father of Carlos. I confirmed an order at once for a male, silver Maine Coon kitten. I had hopes that the new kitten would prove to be an appropriate playmate for Carlos, who, I could often see, became easily bored and frustrated with life.

This decision was to prove more propitious than we could ever have imagined at the time, but for the present life proceeded at the steady uneventful pace of ordinary living except for an extraordinary feat of heroism by Carlos which served to endorse our already developing love for him. The incident happened on one fine summer evening when Catherine and I were relaxing in the garden, enjoying the warm sunlight. We were sitting in the gazebo at the top end of the garden. The weather over the period of the previous two weeks had been extremely hot with little or no wind, a rare condition for the far north-east.

It had become noticeable how insect activity had intensified to the point where we were becoming increasingly wary of wasps, though we had not anticipated large hornets, which inflict a lethal sting for anyone allergic to their poison. Suddenly, a monster black-and-yellow banded hornet appeared and mounted a determined assault on Catherine. It might have been attracted to the scent of soap or perfume on her skin but whatever the cause it had her trapped in the corner of the shelter from which she could not easily escape. Our flapping hands did nothing to dissuade its attack and it began to buzz ominously. All at once, when the offending hornet was barely inches away from her face, a silver streak erupted on to the scene and knocked it to the ground. It was Carlos to the rescue and he now proceeded to whack the disabled insect until it was dead. We were at once relieved and amazed. We had not been aware of Carlos in the proximity – it was just as if he came from nowhere.

Catherine picked him up and gave him a loving hug in gratitude and carried him into the house to give him a treat. Later that evening, as we reflected on his heroism, we elected to award a special medal for him and determined that it should be nothing less than the Owl Cottage Victoria Cross for Cats.

'Do you think he'll understand?' Catherine asked.

'If he could understand that you were in danger and chose to intervene to save you from a very nasty sting then I think he will understand only too well. After all, Maine Coon cats are noted for their intelligence and loyalty to their adopted family. Anyhow, you said he was a commando and that's what commandos do!' I said, praising him.

The next morning Catherine removed his neck collar and sewed a silver star button to it which she had taken from her jewellery box. We arranged to have a special ceremony in the garden in the afternoon, when we would award the medal to Carlos, together with some special teatime treats. Although I know some people would view our actions as being the height of daftness I was aware from my reading that there had been many recorded deeds of heroism by animals, some by cats, which had contributed to saving the lives of humans and we were not going to deny Carlos a well-deserved meritorious award for his bravery.

Catherine concocted an award meal consisting of cold pheasant and turkey. It fell to me to articulate the award ceremony and it amused me to see the look of bemusement on the face of Carlos as I called him to me and the citation was read out to him. I hung his collar with the medal attached around his neck and kissed him on both cheeks as the ritual demanded. Meanwhile, the leonine face of Pablo peeped out from underneath a nearby bush, curious as to what all the fuss was about. Both cats showed no hesitation when presented with the meal, although Carlos only ate half of his and whined for biscuits, which I hurriedly acquired for him. Pablo, ravenous as usual, cleaned off both dishes. The evening ended on a most propitious note and we all retired happily to the cottage.

Good news arrived the next day with a call from Jane to say that her she-cat Florence had given birth overnight to a litter of six healthy kittens, which included a stunningly marked silver grey, the diminutive picture of his dad Oscar, who was mine for the asking. I rang her immediately to claim the kitten and to convey my congratulations to Florence.

Meanwhile, Carlos was showing a much more controlled and disciplined attitude to life and was less inclined to 'rush in where Angels fear to tread', as the saying goes. I was often pleased to see him, whenever we were off on one of our field excursions, wanting to rush away in a particular direction because of something that had aroused his attention. Previously, on occasions such as this, when the mood took him he would tug forwards with such force that I would almost fall over and he would suffer a fit of coughing because the harness had constricted his chest. But now, after all his training, I was glad to see that when he became excited he would turn and look back at me and whine as if he was asking permission. Usually I would say OK and he would lead me to towards whatever interesting scent or sight had attracted his attention.

He showed many other characteristics which were unique to his personality, two of which always made me laugh. Sometimes at the weekend when Catherine drove away on an early shopping expedition, I would allow Carlos to sit on the table near me while I ate a late breakfast. This was a special treat for both of us because I loved his company and it was a secret to be shared between us, a sort of buddy male pact. During this breakfast ritual I would enjoy offering him tasty bits of bacon and sausage. Then Carlos would interact with me in a playful and humorous way. He would lie full length with his face pointing towards me and pretend to be sleeping, only I could detect that he was peeping through his eye slits. Then when he believed I wasn't watching he would slowly extend a paw surreptitiously towards my plate. I would join in this game by permitting him to grab a morsel of bacon, which he would draw back towards him and eat still with his eyes closed. When he tried it again I would give the intrusive paw a rejecting tap. And at this his eyes would jerk open and if a cat could smile he smiled with me. It was fun for both of us.

Then there were times when I would be sequestered in the bathroom of a morning. While carrying out my ablutions, my attention would be drawn to a slight noise by the door. The first time it happened I watched in amazement as a paw covered in silver fur sneaked slyly through the gap under the door and groped around as if it could somehow gain entry. This was Carlos playing another game with me; he was letting me know that he knew I was in there and whatever was going on he wanted to be part of it. Also I believed he was trying to amuse me.

Another fun game we played was when I would suddenly make a dash at him while he was strolling along the hall. Instantly, he would respond in kind and make a mad dash upstairs then turn at the top, staring down at me with ears pricked. If I then ran away in mock fear to the conservatory he would hurtle down and chase me; then I would turn and charge at him again and the game would be repeated. I know it sounds juvenile but we both enjoyed such playtime romps.

He loved playing games with Pablo, usually of the chasing

kind, if the big cat was in the mood. If no one was available to have a play with him he would set about amusing himself and so would give an entertaining display of jumping and pouncing on stray leaves blowing in the wind or a fragment of twig dropped from a tree. I was often drawn away from my writing to watch him from a window, in awe at his capacity for exceptional light-hearted play and gamesmanship. These were memorable moments that I would store forever of a splendid cat called Carlos, of whom I dared ever to say was mine – as if anyone could possess such a free spirit. Unfortunately, our halcyon days were numbered, though neither of us, at that happy time, was to know how it would all tragically end.

The summer had proved to be exceptional and bird life in the garden had flourished, as had the crows nesting in the nearby rookery. I have ambivalent views about the crow family, which includes rooks, ravens, hooded crows and magpies. I know that they serve a useful purpose by disposing of carrion and lots of bugs that inhabit the rural landscape. I also know that they function as an intelligent community from the stories I've heard from farmers and gamekeepers who have told me of crows gathering to punish one of their group who has committed an offence in their colony. Recently, I read in the newspapers of magpies assembling to mourn one of their flock, but I did not credit the crows I see every day with profound emotional attributes until one summer when I witnessed the following incident.

I had observed a man in our community who waged a war

with his shotgun against wildlife in our area. He shot rabbits and hares, and he especially liked to shoot at crows. His killing sprees made me fear for our cats and indeed all cats in the vicinity. I had confronted him once in a field not far from our garden and I warned him about shooting indiscriminately. The more I witnessed this man's activities, the more I grew to dislike him.

One day I heard shotgun bursts coming from the rookery area and I observed the rooks detaching a squadron to circle above the shooter and vent their fury at his intrusions. I spotted him skulking away after failing to kill any of them. Crows are very clever and it is extremely difficult to surprise and kill any of them. But some people fire at their prominent nests built in the tops of the tallest trees in order to destroy the eggs.

It is often my pleasure to watch from our garden what is happening in the district. On a summer morning in June I caught sight of a female crow making an unearthly din from the copse of trees near the front of our cottage. When I investigated I found a huge male crow lying dead on the roadside. It was her mate and he had been shot. I guessed what had happened because in the competition for nesting sites this couple had built their nest in a medium-sized tree overlooking the road, affording the shooter an easy target. I was so angry that I printed notices from my computer declaring this area off bounds to shooting and then telephoned the police about the dangers of shooting near occupied areas, warning them about the man in the village who was the perpetrator.

Sometime later I saw that the lone female crow had reared a chick. She had probably only laid one fertile egg because her mate had been shot before they had got fully going with their mating. It intrigued me as I watched to see how she fussed and fostered the chick. It delighted me each day to observe how mother and son were always close together and often roosted on trees in our garden. She seemed so proud of him and he prospered under the lavish care he was receiving. In the evenings, because the nest was so close to our garden, I could hear their comfort calls as they settled down for the night. One morning I again found the mother crow in great distress and I didn't have to look far to find why. I found her son's body in the back garden. He had probably been shot as he left the nest to follow his mother, who often traversed our garden on her flight path to the farmer's field. I was in a rage and the next time I encountered the man whom I knew was responsible, I berated him angrily and told him that I would report him by name and address to the police.

Meanwhile, as I gathered up the body of the young crow I was impressed by his sleek black feathers, testament to his mother's loving care. She watched me from a nearby branch as I placed his body in the cleft of one of our trees and left her to privately mourn her son. She never left his body for five days and she stroked him with her beak and head, and cried piteously over him as I watched from an upstairs window. Then I decided enough was enough and buried his body in our garden because I could bear her sadness no longer. She watched me as I buried him and, job finished, I called out to her, telling her to make a new life. The next day she'd gone and I never saw her alive again.

It rained heavily in early July and after a few days of torrential downpours our conservatory began to leak. Later that week, during a dry spell, I summoned a builder to do repairs. He only needed a short time to find the cause of our leak. He called me outside to show me the dead body of a crow which had blocked the gutter on the roof, causing a flooding down the wall at the side of the conservatory. I recognized the body at once: it was the bereaved mother crow. Her body was emaciated, as if she'd starved to death. Catherine came out to see what was happening and I showed her the crow's remains.

'What's that?' she said.

'It's the mother crow that I told you about. Look at how emaciated her body is. She must have starved to death because she was pining over the death of her son. Somebody shot him and I watched her as she mourned him. This bird died of a broken heart. Amazing, isn't it? A bird feeling emotional sentiments comparable to humans. What will the cynics say now?'

All my life I have struggled to make people aware of the complexity of nature and how human beings drastically under-estimate the abilities and skills of the wild creatures living around us. Since I was a boy, freely wandering the riverbanks and woods, I have become ever more impressed and enchanted by watching animals going about the business of their daily lives.

Far from being inferior, their capacity to cope with the exigencies of life far outweighs those of some of their human counterparts. In this respect I am constantly overcome with admiration for the qualities shown by cats in their relationships with people as well as the environment.

As June gave way to the promise of a hot July there was much excitement in the cottage because an important birthday was looming. On the 6th of July Carlos would be one year old and what a year it had been. We always celebrate the birthdays of our cats to show how much we love and care for them. I did it for Toby Jug and with our new Maine Coon cats, Pablo and Carlos. We intended to continue the tradition and establish birthday celebrations as an Owl Cottage custom. The day turned out to be fine and sunny with not a cloud in the sky and only a soft breeze slightly stirring the leaves of our trees. Carlos was enthralled to be the centre of attention and rejoiced with mad dashes across the lawns and the feverish scratching of tree trunks. To climax his display he showed how competent he had become in catching and returning small rubber balls we threw for him. Whilst all this activity was proceeding Pablo kept a watchful if sleepy-eyed view of the ceremonies from a thick branch of the old ash tree next to the barbeque area so that he could check what was cooking.

As we all gradually grew tired of playing in the hot sunshine it was, thankfully, time for the birthday tea. We had carefully prepared small pieces from our own barbequed food to entice

Carlos to eat meat. We didn't need to encourage Pablo as he was always up and ready for any meat dish. Catherine was having chicken breast and my preference was a thick sirloin steak. Carlos sniffed at the meat morsels and made a stab at eating some steak, but quickly abandoned the food on offer and stared expectantly at me.

'He's after biscuits,' Catherine said with a sigh because of the worries about his diet.

'I'll get him some,' I said resignedly.

'You spoil him,' she said. Then she burst out laughing because Pablo had jumped down to eat the morsels refused by Carlos. Meanwhile, Carlos was provided with a bowl of the best dry food biscuits we could buy and, as a special treat, a saucerful of tapioca pudding. Later, whilst we washed down our meal with a mug of coffee followed by a glass of wine, the cats retired to a garden bench and engaged in assiduous ablutions by means of prolonged tongue-washes. The day had given us a rare taste of hot summer without a cloud in the sky and now that it was drawing to a close a faintly cooling breeze was most welcome.

The fading sunlight cast golden rays across the freshly mown lawn, irradiating the grass with myriad shades of green and yellow, and as the daylight succumbed to the orange and red glow of sunset we all trooped wearily indoors to relax. It had been a grand day.

It proved to be an excellent week for weather, with sunshine and blue skies. We took advantage of it to carry out some essential gardening tasks. The two cats did their own thing except that Carlos seemed to know whenever I went into the greenhouse because he felt obliged to join me and scrutinize my efforts at pruning the tomato plants. He also liked me to talk to him and he would listen from a reclining position on the potting bench with eyes wide open as if not to miss a single word of my many tales of cats and wild country places.

Outside in the garden the swallows were busy in a frenzy of nest-repairing and mating and, no doubt, we would soon be greeted each morning with the excited calls of nestlings hungry for the next feed. When this time came we needed to warn callers at our front door that there was a swallow family living just above their heads high in the canopy and they could be very aggressive with visitors intruding into their space. Our postman was most at risk because his bald head had to run the gauntlet of their offensive swoops each morning as he delivered the mail. On days when we were at home we felt compelled to offer him the protection of an umbrella and I did promise him a sample of my tomatoes when they ripened as a palliative for his suffering.

Meanwhile, at the back of the cottage the house martins had almost completed their rugby-ball shaped nest of mud and spittle under the overhanging roof outside the window of the spare bedroom. Furthermore, blackbirds had invaded and occupied the ivy-covered wall adjacent to the conservatory, though it was the impudence of a pair of ring doves who had woven their nest into the Sky satellite dish that gave the most cause for amazement. The cats viewed this encroachment of the feathered brethren into our garden territory with steely eyed hostility but had long given up trying to catch the swallows as they swooped and dived in their aerial acrobatics as they took insects on the wing. In the long summer evenings, when we sat in the garden and we witnessed their tireless flights over our heads, I could not avoid thinking, while I listened to their muted calls as they winged their way around, that their vocal outbursts must partly be cries of sheer rapture at the joy of flying.

Saturday morning was golden with the sunshine which had graced every day that week. I had stayed up late to finish some writing so Catherine, who loves to walk through the garden on summer mornings, was first up. Carlos decided to search for me. Suddenly, I was awakened with a start from a deep sleep by a thud on the bed followed by a rasping wet tongue licking my arm and then my face, and finally the sound of loud purring in my ears. Carlos had found me. When he realized I was awake he started pawing the duvet, which was the signal for me to lift it so that he could crawl inside and lie on the sheet against me. As soon as he was between the bedclothes he nestled closer to me and eventually settled on my chest. I was half asleep but felt comforted by his presence so near to me. I decided to doze a while longer. Having completed all his positional manoeuvres he laid his head just below my chin, a mandatory invitation to me to stroke his head, which I duly did even though I was not quite fully awake yet.

I was surprised but pleased that he had remembered this bedroom ploy of his which he had done regularly as a kitten.

He had seemingly abandoned the practice of late when I was working on ways to bond with him. I savoured this intimately private time with him and was proud that he was maturing into such a wonderful cat, bright as a button with a gleaming coat of silver fur set off by the handsome dark leg rings of the true-bred Maine Coon cat. Had I known in advance what this day would bring I would have locked him away until the time passed but, as it is, I have sealed the memory of that morning's togetherness deep in my heart where it lives anew each time I think of him. Not a day passes but for a stray thought that takes me back to my time with Carlos.

We came downstairs and he sat by my chair as I ate a quick breakfast of tea and toast, since we were due to go shopping later that morning. As I showered, shaved and dressed, he sat on the laundry basket to keep me company. Then, as Catherine drove the car out from the garage, I opened the patio door to let Carlos out. It was the last time I saw him alive.

After we had done the shopping we broke for a light lunch at a small restaurant just by the back of the Alnwick Castle walls. It was early afternoon when we arrived home and, after unpacking the shopping, I strolled into the hallway to collect the post. Picking up the letters I noticed a handwritten note lying off to one side. 'Please call round when you get back. I need to show you something.' The note was signed by Julie, our neighbour.

I hastened round to her house to find out what the mystery could be. She spotted my approach and met me by her garage door, which was open. I looked at her and saw that she wore a markedly serious expression so different from her usual smiling greetings and I immediately became worried.

She said, 'I hope I'm wrong but I was walking up the bank with Jane and Clare when we discovered the body of a cat lying in the road. I do hope it isn't yours. It's in the garage.' She spoke quietly as if afraid of what I might find. In a quick movement she opened the garage door wider.

At her words my stomach constricted and my heart began beating wildly as I had an immediate premonition of tragedy. Sure enough, in the bright light from the open door, I saw the body of Carlos, curled unnaturally in the terrible pain of his death throes, lying on Julie's shovel. Feeling an icy dread beyond description, I somehow found the words to thank Julie for recovering his body from the road before the traffic squashed him into something unrecognizable. I picked him up and, cradling his body in my arms, I fled back home and went immediately to the greenhouse where I sat holding his dead body to my chest. I wept and in the weeping I could hear someone making anguished moans until I realized they were coming from me. Eventually, I became aware of Catherine standing in the doorway of the greenhouse. Her face was covered in tears but she tried to help me, knowing how close I had been to Carlos.

'Julie told me about Carlos. Your sweater is covered in blood. Shouldn't we bury him? Come on, Denis. We can't do anything more for him now.'

I heard her as if from a long distance away. I had retreated into a dimension of denial from which I was not prepared to resurface for some time. In my mind I was with Carlos, alive. At last I gave way to Catherine's gentle prodding and reluctantly carried his body to the place where he used to lie in the upper garden and Catherine followed me, carrying my garden spade. I told her to go and get my dark, nearly new fleece from the cupboard upstairs. This was what I had worn when Carlos and I did some of our later excursions together and I remember how he loved to cuddle into its warmth when I held him after our walks back to the car. I wrapped his still beautiful body in my fleece and began to dig his grave. It was as if I was sleepwalking. I can hardly remember the burial except that Pablo was there making hollow-sounding cries that became yowls, and I believe we cried over Carlos together. Before I filled in the grave, from my right wrist I unfastened the silver bracelet which Carlos had loved to grapple with and chew. I dropped it in his grave as a goodbye token of affection from me.

Pablo joined me and together we mourned Carlos at the side of his grave. Pablo whimpered and pawed the grass above the grave and looked up at me in incomprehension.

'I know,' I said to him. 'My heart is broken too; yet again.'

Later I brought a garden chair over to his grave site and mounted a vigil, despite Catherine's protestations. I was still suffering the shock of disbelief and although I had buried him and knew that he was in the grave in front of me, I kept glancing round expecting him to appear. The time passed very quickly and soon the daylight was gone and a pale half-moon appeared.

In the clear night sky, Catherine came out to where I was sitting and tried again to persuade me to come back inside the cottage. I explained that I could not abandon him to the cold ground and the darkness. His spirit would be confused and worried as he'd obviously been killed instantly. If his spirit knew that I was near it would comfort him until he was taken care of.

'I know he loved me and I cannot desert him,' I said with a sob in my voice. I realized that she was also upset at his death but she could handle it better than I could. After all, he had been very much my cat and we had been through a lot together. I missed him and always would. As a testament to this sentiment I carry to this day a photograph of him in my wallet. Sometime later, Catherine brought me a large glass of brandy and a thick blanket and then Pablo, with a soulful look at me, followed her back to the cottage.

Meanwhile, as I sipped the brandy and hugged the blanket for warmth, I viewed in my mind's eye the many memories of my times with Carlos and I softly spoke a message for him to the night sky, trusting that in some way the night would communicate it, telling him that I prayed his spirit would soon find peace and that nothing would ever stop me loving him.

As the first red streaks of the new day dawned Catherine came out in her nightwear and slippers and led me inside. I could not bear to go to bed and simply dozed in an armchair by the fireside. With the death of Carlos something had died within me also. A host of precious feelings had vanished and it reminded me how I had suffered at the death of Toby Jug.

For solace I turned inevitably to music as a balm for my feelings and selected a piece by Maurice Ravel, 'Pavane pour une infante défunte' ('Lament for a deceased princess'), as being the most appropriate, despite being for the wrong gender. After which Mahler and Wagner served to ease my heart somewhat during that first morning without Carlos' company. I found that I couldn't eat and just drank one cup of tea after another while staring out into the garden.

The days that followed the death of Carlos were unbearable for both of us and it was Catherine who suggested that we should plan to get away from the cottage, where everything reminded us of him, and fill our minds with new experiences such as visiting National Trust properties and the like. This strategy worked to a large extent but it would take a long time before I could think of Carlos without feeling pangs of anguish and hurt. Curiously, in the days that followed, both Catherine and I had dreams in which Carlos appeared to us as we had known him in happier times. After the dreams we each remarked how we had felt comforted. A week after I had buried Carlos I visited a builder's yard and selected a large grey stone scored with streaks of silver, which I placed on his grave. On the topside of the stone I scratched his name and dates. He had lived just one year and six days, but in that time he had made his mark and it was for me an unforgettable legacy of high spirits and humorous affection. Catherine and I visited a local garden centre and chose a hybrid tea rose to plant on his grave. It was purple with white and pink flecks of colour. It blooms with abundance each summer and serves as an annual reminder of his beautiful spirit.

LUIS

Now I had to address the problem of whether to accept the silver male kitten which I had ordered to be a playmate for Carlos. I could never ever replace Carlos and it would be folly to try but I now desperately needed a kitten to replace the emotional gap left by his death. Pablo was a fine, loving animal but he had his own, wild-wandering agenda. Perhaps a new little Maine Coon from the same sire and she-cat would have some of the spark and appearance which would remind me favourably of Carlos and console me for his loss.

'I'll know whether I want him when I see him,' I told Catherine as we drove down to Jane's house to meet the new kitten. It turned out to be a much better experience than I had expected. When we arrived Jane was outside, tending her garden. She immediately commiserated with us about the loss of Carlos but then made some interesting comments. She remarked that Carlos had inherited too much of the 'wild side' of cat nature not to act recklessly and to gamble once too often with his life. We met old cat friends like Hamish and Rory, who had matured but did not seem to have aged at all, a testament to Jane's love and care for them.

Becoming impatient I blurted out, 'Well, where is he, then?'

Jane gave me a hard look that was nearly an admonishment.

'You must understand he's no Carlos, but he's one of the handsomest kittens I've ever seen and he's a real little gentleman,' she said, smiling. 'Why don't you go and find him for yourself. He's in there somewhere but you'll need to be polite to him because he's very aristocratic, a real pedigree Maine Coon in more ways than one!'

As instructed I searched the downstairs rooms and came across two dark-grey kittens running about but intuitively knew that neither one was him. I had just begun to climb the stairs when I realized that I'd found him. Sitting upright on a stair looking down at me, with an adopted regal pose that belied his size, was a proud-looking little fellow with azure blue eyes. His gaze settled on me and mine on him and I believe that I was the one most impressed. He possessed that uncanny bearing that some cats have which can make a person feel inferior. In appearance he had a startlingly light-coloured chest. Its curly, silver-white fur gave him the distinctive air of a cavalier such as in oil paintings of the courtiers to King Charles II. The rest of his body was covered in thick silver fur and his bushy tail could have featured in a work of art. I admired his appearance but it was his stance and demeanour that spoke of the genuine thoroughbred strain of the nobility of Maine Coon lineage. Immediately, I was aware of the accuracy of Jane's description. He was exceptional – a fine little gentleman indeed.

As I picked him up he uttered a weeny cry, as if I should have first asked his permission.

'Oh, pardon me, your majesty,' I said to this baby prince. 'But you see we are destined to share life together and I promise to show due care and devotion to you.'

I carried the tiny mite into the garden with me and sat on a rustic garden seat at the far end with him cradled on my chest. In a way that only an animal can accomplish, his close presence began at once to ease and soothe the hurt I was feeling. I stroked his tiny head and body, and spoke to him gently about how I thought our life together might be, how I would take him for walks when he learned to wear a harness and lead, and how he would come with me in the car. Then he did a most extraordinary thing. He was facing away from me but instead of turning to look at me he bent his head back and viewed me from what was for him an upside-down angle. This move astonished me because it was exactly how Carlos had often looked back at me. No other cat I had known had ever done this and I felt that it was a good omen for our future. This kitten was destined to be with us.

I could see that my wife was in earnest conversation with Jane at the bottom of the garden, but she was keenly watching and had missed nothing of my interactions with the kitten.

'Well, your highness,' I said to him, 'please accept me as your loyal guardian and soon you will be welcome to share our wonderful cottage home.'

I needed him and would do my level best to protect him in ways which I was already thinking about, and which I should have done for Carlos. After a brief discussion in the car on the route home we decided to call him Luis, the Spanish form of Louis, in keeping with the Spanish names of the other cats. I also had in mind to pay a token of respect to the memory of the tragic French queen Marie Antoinette, without whose interest in breeding and decision to transport her cats to America Maine Coon cats would never have existed.

At this point I feel the need to express something regarding the sentiments that I hold regarding cats as well as other animals, which I'm sure are shared by many other animal lovers. When I relate to a cat, dog or a horse, for example, I am looking for what kind of personality the animal possesses and then I want to find out whether it is compatible with mine, just as I do when I meet a stranger. When an animal becomes my friend then I will treat it with the affection, respect and courtesy I extend to human friends. It is therefore abhorrent for me to hear other people judge my feelings towards my cats as ridiculously sentimental and out of proportion. As someone remarked to me when I recounted the death of Carlos, 'Well, he was only a damned cat, after all.' This statement implies that animals are not worthy, nor are they capable of sentiments such as love and caring, but the evidence from individuals who share their lives with animals overwhelmingly suggests otherwise.

I am aware that there is an entrenched attitude held by many throughout the world who evaluate animal life only in terms of its usefulness to humankind and who treat cats as vermin. Once I lectured to an industrial conference in Benidorm, Spain, and it was there that I encountered the latter. It was in the early

and Luis's presence started a healing process both for Catherine and for me. He was a delight to have with us and we played the usual kitten games with him, dangling strings with bits of paper attached for him to jump at, but there was a marked difference in his behaviour from other cats we had lived with. For one thing he was so self-assured and independent-minded even at the age of twelve weeks. He was dignified to the point of appearing haughty. He gave me the impression that he was well aware that the Ancient Egyptians had venerated cats as gods and, indeed, believed the practice should be reinstated. I marvelled at his regal posture and worried that the way he looked denoted such a sense of superiority that I would never be able to get really close to him. The established *modus operandi* in his opinion seemed to be that we belonged to him rather than the other way around. I gathered that he had made up his mind to adopt us but only so long as he remained the Little Master.

'We'll have to see about that,' I thought, but then I have always believed all cats, even as kittens, come into this world with readymade agendas. Their willingness to modify their plans depends upon with whom they strike up a relationship. I would need to gently go to work on Luis as soon as possible or else I could envisage him becoming one of those lap-cats who take on the aloof disposition of a martinet who rules the roost – that would not permit of a fun, loving bond with a person. I was aware that some such situations had occurred with high-born thoroughbred cats, dogs and horses, perhaps through the emotionally negligent attitudes of the owners towards these animals, and I was determined not to allow this to happen with Luis or we would end up being treated as his servants. I was to learn more about this side to Luis' personality when we returned to Jane's home for his final injections.

We arrived early and Jane invited us to have some tea. Meanwhile, Luis was turned loose to rejoin the other five kittens in his litter. As usual Hamish came to inspect us but now that he knew us he was quite satisfied with just a cursory sniff at our shoes. Whilst Catherine and Jane chattered I watched the kittens. Seemingly the other kittens from the litter recognized Luis at once and treated him as something of a celebrity, which suited his ego no end. They gathered around him and gave him a good sniff all over, which was their way of saying: 'Where have you been these past ten days and what have you been doing?' After a while some of the kittens began to give him a tongue-wash, especially over his head and neck. I was intrigued to watch this behaviour because, whilst having this beauty treatment lavished upon him, he literally lorded it over the other kittens and adopted a pose which I can only describe as the 'Little Monarch'. The surprising thing about it was that the others seemed to accept Luis as their sibling superior.

Finally, it was time for Jane to take the litter down to the vet's for their final injections. The kittens were bundled into a secure carrying box and off she went in her car, accompanied by Catherine, while I stayed behind to 'hold the fort'. Soon I was surrounded by the mature cats of the household and I paid especial attention to Florence, Luis' mother, a beautiful silver she-cat who eagerly devoured some of the cat biscuit treats I always carry in my pocket. Then Hamish, the huge sable and brown tabby, the alpha male, ambled over to enjoy a handful. By this time the gang from the vet's arrived back in the midst of a drenching downpour and for a time there was a deal of fussing and disturbance until the adults dried off and the hungry kittens were released for a light supper.

We said our goodbyes and Jane told us to bring the car near to the gate and she would carry Luis out to us. It had grown dark outside and the pelting rain forced us to make a mad dash for our car, which I had parked further down the street. As I drove up the car headlights picked out Jane standing by her garden gate, a raincoat over her head and holding a wriggling kitten in her arms. Catherine opened her side window and took hold of the kitten from Jane. Then we were off homewards with the windscreen wipers on full power. In the faint light from the dashboard I kept shooting sideways glances at the kitten on Catherine's knee and I became increasingly disturbed. I could not recognize the kitten as Luis; as far as I could see it did not have such a light breast and there were no racoon-like dark rings on its front legs, which were a distinct feature on Luis. Convinced we had the wrong kitten I stopped the car and put on the interior light. Then, removing the kitten from Catherine's lap, I held it up for a closer examination. At this intrusion the kitten, which must have been afraid anyway, went berserk and raked my bare arm with its claws, drawing blood. I set it down and turning to Catherine said, 'This is not our kitten; I'm going back.'

'Are you really sure?' she said.

'Positive.'

Reversing the car I arrived back at Jane's house, where she was most surprised to see me.

'You gave us the wrong kitten; go out to the car and see for yourself,' I said, marching indoors. I looked around and began calling his name loudly. At once three kittens charged towards me with Luis in the centre. I picked him up and made sure that it was definitely him. All these kittens were due to go to their new homes on the morrow and if I took the wrong kitten home I would never see Luis again.

Just then Jane rushed in. 'The kitten in the car is definitely yours, Denis,' she cried.

'No, Jane, this is my Luis,' I said adamantly, holding him up for her to see.

'Oh!' she exclaimed. 'I must have given you the "she".'

'You'd better go and get her because she's not at all fond of me.' And here I proffered my scratched and bloodied arm for her to see. Of course, I did not blame the kitten. She must have been terrified at being taken away in the dark and manhandled by me, someone she didn't even know.

Jane soon returned, having retrieved the other kitten from the car. 'Sorry!' she murmured.

'Well, it's alright now,' I said, heading out to the car with Luis in my arms, feeling angry but vindicated.

The rest of the journey home was uneventful except for the atrocious weather. This time Luis sat on my knee and kept raising his head to look up at me as if to say, 'Why did you leave me and did you know my two brothers wanted to come as well?' I chuckled at my fanciful imaginings and found that my anger had totally dissipated.

Soon life at the cottage settled into tranquil bliss once more and my energies were focused on habituating Luis to our way of life. The heartache of the recent tragedy would never be forgotten but through time would be filed away in that special inner mind that helps us to cope with sorrows that would otherwise drive us mad.

During this time I was thinking carefully of what I could do to avoid losing Luis in the precipitous way that Carlos had died. Eventually, we decided that we had a large enough garden to build a compound wherein Luis and any other cats we acquired would be safe from killer traffic and yet be free to roam around trees and bushes in a limited area. Of course, I intended to train Luis to walk wearing a harness and lead like Carlos had done and would take him on excursions into the wilds of Northumberland. He would also spend an appreciable amount of time with us in the house. This was the best compromise I could think of to keep my cat safe and it matched the expressed current wisdom on keeping thoroughbred cats of any species.

To this end I contacted a man called Alan who worked as a carpenter for the Estates Office of the Duke of Northumberland. At that time he was a member of the team building a massive treehouse feature which was to enclose a restaurant in the

Alnwick Gardens Complex being developed by the Duchess of Northumberland. Alan proved to be a very great help and built a large square enclosure in the upper part of the garden, shielded by trees. Inside, the compound had high runs, balconies and shelves from which a cat could survey the world around him and feel part of the natural environment. A mature lilac and a bamboo tree, together with the grave of Carlos and his rosebush, were enclosed by the walls made from wood and chicken wire. High up in a roofed alcove, Alan built a long shelf which was protected from the weather. In this area I placed two large wooden hutches, one lying on top of the other. These had both indoor and outdoor compartments and were filled with cushion-beds and warm blankets to equip the facility with protection in cold weather. There was an outer and inner door for security and to prevent escape at our comings and goings with food and water.

All together it proved to be the ideal solution of where to house the cats when they were not with us in the cottage. It also afforded the cats with an exercise area and somewhere from which to view the garden and avail themselves of some fresh air in addition to their walks with us. It would provide a place of interest for Luis and we could also put Pablo inside as a precautionary measure to stop him wandering abroad and being at risk during the day, since he preferred that we let him out at night.

Now that the compound was built I could turn my attention to studying and befriending Luis. He really was a most interesting and adorable little fellow, entirely different from other cats I had known. Much in keeping with his aura of royalty, he was more than normally fastidious about his appearance, always tongue-washing and preening himself; he was also fussy about where he lay or sat. He preferred perfect conditions wherever possible and liked to sit on our chairs rather than the cushion-beds that we provided for him that smelled of the other cats who had used them.

My attempts to introduce him to wearing a harness and walking on a lead as early as feasible illustrated this aspect of his character. Pablo and Carlos had at first belligerently objected to wearing a harness. But not Luis. He stoically suffered the fitting around his body of the straps in dignified silence and trotted around the garden as if he had been born to it, almost as if it was beneath his high breeding to create a fuss. In this respect he reminded me of Toby Jug, who never fussed about wearing a harness and walking on a lead whenever I decided that it was necessary for his safety. It was at this point that I really began to be impressed by Luis and decided that this kitten was worthy of admiration.

As time passed we grew to know our new kitten better and to appreciate some of his foibles. For example, one day Catherine took him for an introductory walk around our garden with me trailing behind. Earlier in the day there had been a light shower and the ground was still damp. Luis did not like this at all and kept stopping to raise his paws and hind feet to shake off the moisture. When the walk reached the shelter of the gazebo

Catherine was astonished to observe Luis doing the exact same thing as Carlos had done in similar circumstances. He shook his paws, licked them clean and climbed on to the instep of Catherine's shoe so that none of his feet touched the ground, mimicking, just as Carlos had done, the image of the polar bear standing on top of a Fox's Glacier Mint sweet. It made us both laugh and also wonder at the power of the genes to affect behaviour in similar fashion to his half-brother. He then looked up at her and whined his irritation. We wished we'd had a camera to hand as it would have made an amusing picture. Luis' endeavours to remain not only high and dry but regal at all times gave us some hilarious moments, but he would glare at us with annoyance if we laughed at him too openly.

Alongside this princely air that Luis adopted there existed an attribute to his personality which was very reserved; he was a most introverted cat. I sympathized with him totally when I realized that this little cat needed quiet time to himself; he wanted to be alone. He reminded me of myself and he was most unlike Carlos. One morning when I had him on my knee and was quietly talking to him and gently stroking his fur he suddenly broke away and trotted across the room to where a small footstool lay underneath an easy chair. He climbed on to the stool and folded himself into a comfortable position with his front paws tucked under his body in the posture that all cats adopt, which we call 'Little Hen'. With his eyes wide open he sat there as if meditating on cat issues and other things.

I thought about it for a while as I silently studied him and began to understand that Luis craved the opportunity to be by himself as a necessary condition to enable him to cope with the world. This feature of his behaviour was repeated on many occasions over the weeks following his arrival at Owl Cottage, when he would secrete himself away somewhere, preferably dark and quiet, in a cupboard or behind the sofa, somewhere where he wouldn't be disturbed. When he'd had enough of this time on his own he would reappear and join our company. At first I played along with this, not wishing to aggravate him and lose his friendship, but then I began to think that perhaps he was overdoing it and it wasn't healthy for him. Whereas Carlos could rarely bear to sit quietly by himself without intermittently jumping into action, Luis liked attention but he preferred it to be his idea: he would choose the time when he would come to us to be fondled and stroked. His enthusiasm for life was muted and contemplative rather than the gung-ho approach displayed by Carlos.

In view of this I began to think carefully about how I could win his confidence and bond him to me like my other cats, because I needed to have a close relationship with any cat of mine or I didn't feel right. After pondering the situation at some length I made up my mind to employ the simplest tactic, one used for thousands of years as a means of taming and domesticating animals: I would feed him by hand. Since I am in the habit of writing late into the night and early morning it is usually Catherine who arises first and feeds the cats. I told her of my plan and asked her not to feed Luis with Pablo but to leave Luis for me. I thought that this would give him time to think and perhaps search me out for a solution.

The very first morning this happened I was awakened by a diminutive figure at my bedside making cries of protestation which I knew only too well from experience with my other cats. He was obviously worried and wanted me to do something about it. I walked downstairs accompanied by a small silver cat in a high state of panic who anxiously paced the kitchen and fretfully circled my feet making hoarse squawks of hunger as I brewed my morning cup of tea. Mug of tea in hand, I pretended to ignore him. His majesty was not accustomed to being treated this way. Seated at the table, having my bowl of cereal, I had to hide a grin as Luis scrambled on to one of the chairs and thence advanced tentatively towards me. Stopping at a respectful distance from my plate he gave me a fraught look that conveyed fully his dissatisfaction with events and he whined to my face.

'Sorry, Your Majesty,' I said, 'but you will have to make a much greater effort to be friendly if you want matters to improve.'

At this point Catherine intervened and stated firmly that she thought that I was tormenting the kitten and she would have nothing to do with it. I patiently explained that I wanted to win him over to become closer to me and to bring out his affectionate side. She looked at me disapprovingly, picked up the kitten and took him away to give him some comfort. But no sooner had she taken him into the study and set him on her lap then I heard her cry out and Luis came scrambling back on to the table and blankly stared at me. I knew that I had read somewhere that it is virtually impossible for a person to outstare a cat but I fixed my eyes on him and stared back. Then he did a surprising thing. He got up and came to me and purred. I then realized that he had shifted into manipulatory mode. I could feel his brain ticking over as he thought how best to relate to me in order to get me to do his bidding, which, after all, is what humans are for, only this one had not got the message. Therefore, he had to think again and try a little tenderness.

I reached out and stroked his elegant head and told him that I wanted us to be good friends. I continued staring at him and kept repeating the words, 'Luis, be my friend!' I knew that cats can pick up thoughts and I hoped the message would get through. Then I cleared away my dishes and left the cottage to go to the greenhouse and tend to my tomato plants. As I walked up the garden path I looked back and saw the figure of Luis gazing out from the conservatory door watching me intently. 'Well,' I said to myself, 'that will give him food for thought.'

Busy with my plants I was surprised to be interrupted by Catherine carrying Luis, whom she plonked on to the bench in front of me. 'He's been crying at the door for you so start making friends in here like you did with Carlos. And go easy on him – he's only a baby.' And with that she stormed out, sliding the door shut and leaving us together. Of course, she was right. There were other less harsh ways to break the ice between myself and an aloof and standoffish cat, as cats are traditionally accustomed to be, but not in my cottage and not with me. However, it often takes a woman to sort things out, so I took the hapless new kitten of mine and cuddled him to my chest and when he started to struggle to be free I continued to hold him until he sighed and just slumped against me. I did not get much work done on my plants but I felt that Luis and I were drawing closer to an understanding. I was seeking to arouse the powerful instinct for survival which is designed to make animals search for food and I wanted him to know that making friends with me was the path towards achieving what he wanted. I knew that very soon Luis would engage his super Maine Coon intelligence and figure out how he could get me to feed him. I desired our relationship to be warm and friendly rather than stroppy and distant.

Deciding that he'd suffered enough I took him with me into the cottage and under the critical eye of Catherine I opened the refrigerator and brought out some cold chicken. Meanwhile, Luis was circling my feet and brushing against my legs affectionately. Obviously he had worked out that I was the one to win over if he wanted to be fed. I lifted him on to the kitchen bench and, cutting slivers of chicken breast as I had done for Carlos, I offered to hand-feed him. He hesitated to take them from my hand. He could smell the chicken and wanted some but was baffled at my refusal to give it to him in the normal way, in his bowl. He looked up at me and whined. I gently encouraged him with soft words and dangled the chicken before him. Gathering his courage he lurched forward and snatched the chicken from my hand.

'Come on Luis, have some more,' I said and over the next few minutes he consumed all the chicken I had prepared for him, even forgetting to back away from me each time I fed him another piece. 'Good boy!' I called to him. When he'd finished he lay down on the floor not far from me and tongue-washed his paws and face and, now and again, shot a furtive glance in my direction, since I purposefully did not move but sat near him.

'Well, it's remarkable what a little psychology can do,' I thought to myself. Finally, I said, addressing him directly, 'I think, Your Highness, together we have made some progress today.' He stared at me for a long moment in the way that cats do when they are thinking hard about something, whereas I could not help being impressed at what a lovely little creature he was with his large bewitching eyes, huge for a kitten, and his coat of fur so strikingly marked in silky silver and grey. After that day's lesson had been learned Luis found no problem with feeding from my hand and to reinforce this behaviour I fed him a variety of cooked meats as well as chicken and departed for a while from the usual tinned cat food. Pablo received the same, his share in the normal way in his bowl. In addition both cats had access to a large bowl of dry biscuits. I continued to feed Luis in this fashion for the next month until I gauged that the intended bonding with Luis had been begun successfully, although there was still some way to go before we could be called friends and normal routine feeding procedures with him could be resumed.

During the hand-feeding period I was startled to be awakened early one morning by a robust small body treading my shoulder with needle-sharp claws. Strangely, it was Luis, come to give me a wake-up call despite the fact, unknown to him, that I had worked at my writing until after 4 a.m. Through half-closed eyes I stroked and welcomed him and then relapsed into a deep sleep. Awakening several hours later I felt a warm lump resting between my arm and my chest; it was Luis curled up against me inside the bedclothes. Immediately to my stupefied brain came the revelation that this cat, like all the others I had known and loved, was somehow making it all right. He wanted to show me that there was no need for extraordinary tactics to affect a relationship and that a cat will decide in its own good time when to bond to a human – that it can not be rushed, especially if it is Maine Coon cat. Of course, an alternative explanation could be that he was looking for a warm comfortable berth and my bed suited his purpose. Probably there was a little of both desires in his action.

There remained moments when I felt that I couldn't get close to him but I kept trying. He was still in the habit of sometimes retiring to his seat on the footstool under the chair. I decided to see if I could reach out to him with friendship at such moments. The tactic I adopted was to lie stretched out on the floor close to him and again sweetly to implore him to 'be my friend.' For a few days he ignored me but eventually he graced my efforts one morning by leaving his stool and coming close to me. He licked my face and began to purr as he rubbed against me and I felt elated that I'd made a breakthrough with him. But strangely he would not let me stroke him then nor when he was eating.

During this initial period of our friendship I made a point of taking him for a walk around the garden on his harness lead, encouraging him to investigate the different plants; this was the time when he showed me another aspect of his personality. He loved flowers. Whenever we came near one of the flower beds so carefully laid out by Catherine, Luis would bury his face, eyes closed in ecstasy, into the flowering blooms. Then he would flip on to his back and roll amongst them, which did not do a great deal for the flowers, though I did not stop him because he was so enjoying himself. After the walks I would leave him for a while shut in the newly erected compound so that he could acquaint himself with the area. He proved to be fond of the bamboo tree growing in there and he liked to hide himself within the dense foliage. I was glad for him that he could feel the breath of the breeze stirring his fur and that he could look out to the trees and the grassed areas and become aware of the massive, clear blue Northumbrian sky that overlooked his green space. I left him there for half-an-hour, then brought him back to the house.

Catherine met us at the door saying, 'I hope you're not going to put him through all those expeditions that Carlos had to suffer.'

In reply I could only say that Carlos gained many benefits from our forays into the countryside at large, which made him a more amenable cat with whom to live. Anyway, no matter how I tried I could not bring Luis to accept travelling in the car. He blankly refused to respond and simply moaned all the time. At that time I thought, 'Oh, for the adaptability of Toby Jug, who proved to be such a superior cat.' Although Luis and I gradually became closer I could never persuade him to retrieve objects thrown for him as Carlos had done. They had looked alike in colouring but they were obviously very different-natured cats.

Then all at once things changed for the better. After all my efforts to develop a close bonding with Luis, it happened. He began to accompany me wherever I went in the cottage and remained near when I was doing even mundane things such as hanging a picture frame or fitting batteries to remote controls or torches. He regarded it as a special treat to join me in my efforts at watercolour painting. He would position himself alongside me and all the equipment, and indicate that he wished to investigate every item that I was using. He did this by means of his nose, sniffing out the scents of both the delectable and the bland with equal concentration. He directed his curiosity to all the utensils I used: the paint blocks, the brushes, pens and watercolour pencils. Then he would explore the array of water jars, sometimes helping himself to a drink and occasionally stirring a jar with a paw, if the water had become coloured by washing brushes, to see if it contained anything interesting. During these painting sessions he would stay beside me, watching keenly my every move, apart from snatching a quick snooze when he felt that matters had reached a boring stage. I talked to him a lot of the time but we savoured the long silences together because, for cats as well as for me, silence is a prerequisite for thinking as well as being a personal indulgence. It felt grand to have his company and I realized with relief that he had finally and wholeheartedly adopted me.

He had learned by now that I favoured the rare times when he would join me in bed in the morning to celebrate the start of a new day together. I would tickle and stroke him and he would lie on his back in ecstasy and wriggle to prompt further attention. He especially liked to be stroked on his forehead and to have his nose rubbed. He was developing into a fun cat to be with and I began to feel for him a semblance of that love and true esteem which I had felt for his half-brother Carlos. What a shameful tragedy it was that I couldn't have enjoyed seeing them alive at the same time. Throughout it all Luis never lost the poise and grand look of being a royal thoroughbred of cats and it was heartening to be accepted as a friend of this noble and courtly feline.

He began to show me in numerous little ways that he appreciated my devotion to him by purring when we met, by licking the back of my hand and by making cat-talk to me, which consisted of a series of soft meows accompanied by much side-rubbings of his body against my shins. It was clear that our attachment was reciprocal. But it is strange to recount that I have never quite got rid of the impression that I am his subject, a sort of equerry, a courtier, although I admit that I have sometimes felt this with my other feline friends. Whilst Luis is a cat like any other cat, only more so, I am aware that befriend-ing a cat is not an easy thing to achieve even though it has always been my aim from childhood onwards to relate in a friendly manner to any cat I might encounter in my travels. In the many houses that I visited as a child I chanced upon many house cats who were there to prevent the incursions of mice but although they were freely given a home to share with the family they were in fact strangers to each other and very few people seemed motivated to improve the status quo. What an opportunity they missed. To gain the love of a cat is a most enriching and uplifting achievement and not to be viewed lightly.

Now, there are numerous times when Luis would deliberately initiate contact with me. I may have been reading in the study or working on my laptop when he would suddenly appear and want to make contact. All cats are curious, it is part of their God-given nature, but I found that Luis increasingly directed his inquisitive senses at me. Sometimes he would stride up to me as I worked on my computer and he would, as my American friends are accustomed to saying, 'eyeball' me, probing me with his huge, beautiful, lucid eyes, trying to puzzle out in his cat mind what kind of person I am. He knew that I wasn't a cat and this perplexed him because I should not have been able to affect him in the ways that I had done. In his mind it was perfectly clear that cats, especially himself with a father as illustrious as Oscar, were far superior to humans and only deigned to allow them to serve all their needs. Yet somehow this man had found a way to manipulate cats and that should not be possible. Luis the Magnificent was being controlled and dominated by feelings of closeness to and for this human. It was very perplexing for Luis to work out even though he showed a degree of mental sentience beyond the usual level for a cat.

There exists a strongly held belief among travellers that cats possess psychic capabilities, can facilitate omens of the future and even have powers of divination. I have always felt that my cats have faculties of comprehension beyond my own, as well as superior senses, especially of sight and hearing. I feel a close attachment to cats but I am reluctant to boast that I understand them. Many of them I have loved as friends and in return been loved by them, but I have failed to figure out their precise place in the grand order of things, probably because I am simply human.

It would appear from an article in the *Daily Telegraph* (on Friday, 29 June 2007), which originated in the *Journal of Science*, that a genetic study has provided DNA evidence which suggests that cats probably became domesticated by farming people living in the Middle East around 130,000 years ago. They were attracted to human settlements because of the presence of rodents such as mice and rats which fed upon the farming produce. When some farmers migrated elsewhere they would bring their cats with them. In contrast, an earlier DNA study showed that dogs originated from Asian wolves a mere 15,000 years ago. This means that cats have lived alongside humans for a lengthy period of time in which opportunities to get to know each other really well have been abundant, and yet there still remains an unfathomable distance between the two. On the other hand a dog is much easier to know and to understand. Is this possibly why we regard cats as enigmas and have in the past raised their kind on a pedestal?

It depends on how far a person and a cat are willing to share life as to whether they will become close enough to begin to know each other and to develop a degree of friendship based upon the individual dispositions of both. But where there is determination, as in my case, and the motivating curiosity of the cat, as with Luis, then it is possible that a person and a cat can not only become friends but also end up devoted to each other. The relationship between Luis and myself reached that ideal stage at the beginning of May at the time of his first birthday which Catherine and I celebrated with him in true Owl Cottage fashion. It is interesting to reflect after all my efforts that Luis loves me despite his innate cat nature, which is profoundly committed to his own independence and only allows for contact of a mutually beneficial kind. Cats are instinctively programmed to be their own person, a singularity that permits no adulteration by other species. It required great emotional effort on my part to breach this implacable wall of self-defence against intrusion. In the case of Luis it was formidable, though with other cats of my acquaintance, less so.

After we had started to depend on each other for affection and day-to-day friendship, Luis began to reveal some intriguing aspects of his personality. For one thing he could move as swiftly and as silently as a ghost. When we were all relaxing by the fire in the sitting room of an evening, I might rise and head for the bathroom, only to be beaten there by Luis. He would get up from a state of deep sleep to outpace me so that he could be waiting for me, perched on the washing basket, before I had time to close the door. How he managed to get past me I shall never know. This incredible skill of being able to bypass me without my being aware led me to start referring to him as the Silver Ghost. But this skill of his was superseded by his ability to open doors. Cupboards, wardrobes, kitchen cabinets and kitchen doors left partially unlatched were no problem to this Raffles of a cat. Inevitably, this skill sometimes led him to become imprisoned and it was only after his high-pitched wailing penetrated the broadcasts of the radio or television that we grew aware of his predicament and could mount the rescue of a rueful cat who never seemed to learn his lesson. On one occasion this proclivity of his led to him being incarcerated all afternoon in a spare bedroom whilst we searched the garden and surrounds, thinking he had escaped.

Most of the time Luis was in the cottage, rather than outside, because he would join me in the study where I was writing at my laptop. His presence there became so regular that I bought him an extra cushion-bed and placed it on the shelf by the window so that he could snooze whilst I wrote, though I was aware that his attention always centred on what I was doing. If I left the room for a short while I would return to find him alert and standing, wondering what I had been doing and where I had been. Once a cat makes up its mind about something, nothing will change it. Luis had decided in his mind that he and I were bonded together now and it therefore followed that we would never be separated. Since Luis had abandoned his natural cat attitude of independence he could, and indeed did, demand all the love and devotion that I could give to him in return. I was very willing to do this.

The poignant nature of this relationship was illustrated one day when I drove off to do some specialist shopping and, because of circumstances beyond my control, returned very late. Catherine had brought Luis down from the compound into the cottage, which I usually did. When he could not find me he went berserk. Whining and wailing he paraded the cottage with angry outbursts of suffering at my absence. This behaviour not unnaturally alarmed and distressed her. She began thinking that the cat knew something that she did not and she worried in case something bad had happened to me. Meanwhile, Luis continued his agitation, running here and there in the house and checking all the rooms to try to find me. Cats are conservative in their habits and do not take readily to change; they like an established routine and become stressed when a pattern is not adhered to. Also, and this did not impress upon me until I thought about it later, Luis and I had become very close of late and the cat actually missed me because he had come to rely on me being there for him. Anyone who has viewed the desperate anxiety on a dog's face as they wait, tied to a rung outside the doors of a supermarket, will understand that animals are as vulnerable to feelings as are humans. It was a joyful reunion Luis and I had when at last my car drove up to the cottage. Catherine said that he appeared ecstatic with excitement when he saw me through the window of the conservatory and kept running along the window ledge uttering little cries of what she took for relief.

This episode touched me deeply and I made sure that I allowed time that evening to make a great fuss of him. I also coaxed Catherine to allow me to cut him a piece of her prized Welsh cheddar cheese, for which he'd developed a craving. In fact, he liked all cheddar cheese but Welsh cheddar was his favourite. His taste for food chiefly centred on what he saw me eating and he delighted in cadging morsels of meat from my plate and he was ecstatic when I shared a pork pie snack with him in the garden.

As we increasingly grew to know him, Luis revealed other traits of personality which showed the aesthetic side of cat nature. He enjoyed soft music but ran away from loud orchestral pieces. He dreaded the sound of the huge wagon which emptied the refuse bins and at the first sign of it he would go and hide in a dark corner. Once I followed him to give him comfort and was shocked to find him trembling fitfully. Maine Coon cats do exhibit a lot of delicate sensitivities. When I gave the matter some thought I began to empathize with my cat. While working at a university which was situated in the centre of a city, I became inured to the roar of heavy traffic and accustomed to wending my way though noisy crowds of people whenever I ventured out, but I never liked it. When I escaped through retirement to the sanctuary of rural life I became enamoured once more of waking up to birdsong and the sound of the breeze rustling through the trees. It was also a blissful moment when, on one of my first nights back at Owl Cottage, I saw the stars shining against a backdrop of black sky untainted by pollution. Thinking about all this made me realize how my cats felt. To a cat, sudden noise is an abomination and silence is not only golden, it is divine – a sentiment that mirrors my own feelings precisely.

After a while it became clear to us that Pablo and Luis merely tolerated each other, but sometimes not even that. The harmony of the home would be upset by spats of spitting, hostile cries and growls. While Luis did not appear to be unduly lonely, he did watch our departure in the car for an evening out with a forlorn look as he peeped through the conservatory blinds. We decided that we ought to have another cat to keep him company. And this is how it came about that we acquired Max.

MAX

Following the usual procedure when we wanted a new kitten, I telephoned Jane, the breeder, and asked her what she had available. Jane quickly replied with the good news that she had a pregnant tortoiseshell-coloured cat which had been sired by Oscar, the father of both Carlos and Luis, who was about to give birth any day now. However, her kittens would not be silver-grey but more likely red or pied in colour. She promised to ring and give us first choice when the litter arrived. Two days later she rang to tell us that a litter of two healthy kittens had arrived; one was a deep red with some white markings and the other was black with white mottling. Both kittens were male. We asked her to reserve the red kitten for us and arranged a date for us to see him.

Three-and-a-half weeks later we arrived at Jane's house to view our red kitten for the first time. The twin kittens were cuddled together asleep in a small cosy box, lined with a blanket, on the top of a pedestal. I lifted out the red kitten, which was just a tiny ball of red fur with minute white feet and a little white chest. I carried him into Jane's conservatory to show him to Catherine. Like all our kittens, he was perfectly formed and appeared so vulnerable and endearing as I held him close to my sweater. I stroked him gently with my fingers and he gave two faint squeaks as he viewed me apprehensively with his eyes sparkling like diminutive sapphires. Catherine was anxious to hold him so I laid him in her lap.

'We're going to call him Max,' she said, addressing Jane who had brought in two steaming mugs of coffee as warmers against the cruel January weather. Then a surprising thing happened. We suddenly heard a slight hiss, repeated several times, which sounded as if it was coming from the kitten, which Catherine was now holding up to her face in order to take a good look at him. Sure enough it came again: 'Pith . . . pith . . . pith.'

'This little chap is spitting at me,' laughed Catherine. 'And he's wriggling to be away,' she said as she set him down, only to see him run off. I followed him as he scuttled across the floor into the next room and clambered up the pedestal to rejoin his brother in their box. There they lay cosily cuddled into one another, reminding me of the story of *The Babes in the Wood*, so cute did they look. Catherine had followed me into the room and we both laughed at the sight of the comfy kitten twins soundly sleeping just like babies without a care in the world. But ominously in view of later circumstances we should have afforded these events more significance. If we had, we concluded with hindsight, Max would have had a much less traumatic life than he suffered. At the time we failed to realize, in spite of our experience, that cats, like many other animals, retain strong feelings of belonging to their family, especially certain siblings. It later transpired that in this case the twin brothers were emotionally bonded and as such were inseparable. They were Christmas infants, having been born during the night of 28 December 2002.

It seemed that the winter that year, although severe as always with heavy snowfalls and raging blizzards, passed us by so quickly that we were greeting the spring before we'd had time to prepare a welcome by organizing all the jobs we had to do in the garden and greenhouse. Spring happened so suddenly one golden morning that it seemed that nature had caught everyone unawares. Suddenly the flowers were blooming in plots of brilliant colour and the songbirds were frenziedly nest-building. It was also time to collect our fourth Maine Coon kitten, who had been given the quaint full name of Maxamillion. This is how Jane had printed his pet name on the pedigree certificate and we both laughed about the misspelling but inwardly hoped that it would prove prophetic. We arranged to collect him in the early afternoon. On arrival at Jane's house we were surprised to find her just driving up. As she got out of the car we saw that she was carrying a box and inside was Max. We followed her inside the house where she explained.

'I've had a really bad morning with this one. He's been crying and squirming about as if in pain so I rushed him down to the vet's but it seems as if there is nothing wrong with him as far as they could tell at the clinic,' she ended breathlessly. She went on to tell us that she had rearranged everything in the room where the kittens had been because Max's twin brother had gone to an owner in Glasgow the night before and she wanted to give the room a good cleaning. 'Perhaps shifting everything around upset him but I knew you were coming to get him today and I wanted to get on with reorganizing things.'

We nodded in agreement with her and gave her the cheque in payment for Max but not before thanking her for taking such great care of him. Jane is one of those dedicated breeders who give their all to raising magnificent kittens for the rest of us to enjoy. She coddles her female cats and acts as midwife during their pregnancy and delivery, for which she has all my admiration. We bade her a brisk farewell and, with Catherine cuddling Max on her lap, we drove homewards.

From that moment of departure, we started to develop an acute awareness that Max was suffering some deep distress. At first we put this down to all the changes over the past day or two and the trauma of a visit to the vet. But when we arrived back at the cottage he behaved as if everything was a threat to him and no amount of stroking and gentle talk made the difference. When we put him down on the floor in the conservatory to give him a chance to investigate his new home he withdrew to a corner and as we approached him he began to shake uncontrollably. As you might imagine, this behaviour by our new kitten really upset us and we wondered if we should take him back to Jane to ease his agony. We decided to leave him alone for a while to see if he would calm down. From a distance I watched him keenly for any improvement in his condition but all I could discern was a frightened and miserable kitten. I thought that if I put some food down for him – meat and biscuits with a bowl of water – it might help to comfort him, but he showed no interest in any of it. Eventually we left him alone, huddled in a corner under a chair in the conservatory, and reflected on the marked differences of our four Maine Coon cats. We left the door to the hall open for him to see if he would come and join us. I withdrew to ponder the situation, to see if I could find an explanation and a way to help him.

It was almost an hour later that we began to hear, from the hallway, a series of plaintive wails and cries that pained me to hear. I knew it to be a cat, or rather a kitten, sobbing his heart out. Catherine moved before I could and returned with Max in her arms, trying to mother him and soothe him as she would with one of her own babies. I looked on, feeling totally impotent and worried about how I could possibly relieve this poor kitten's anguish. The sounds emitted from Max indicated that he was consumed with grief for reasons we could not fathom. He shunned all my efforts to comfort him and I could see that Catherine was becoming weary with the effort of trying to ease him, like when all one's efforts to nurse a crying baby are to no avail. We sat with him in the sitting room of the cottage, wondering over and over again what we could do to relieve this lovely kitten of his suffering. At last, exhausted and tormented by his feelings, he fell into a troubled sleep in which he trembled and whimpered, lying with his head resting on Catherine's shoulder, facing her neck. When we were ready for bed we took him up to the bedroom with us and laid him in one of the cushion-beds used by Luis. He lay flat-out, totally comatose.

The next morning he took a long time to rouse himself but

would not move from the cushion, which we had carried downstairs with him in it, and he refused to eat anything even though we offered him every enticement we could think of. On the previous night I had deliberately kept the other cats apart from the kitten, but after Luis had finished his breakfast I brought him into the room where the kitten lay bedfast. I wanted to see if the presence of another cat would revive him and relieve his homesickness, if that was what was troubling him. Luis approached Max tentatively at first and there was a lot of cautious sniffing as the new member of the family was given a thorough appraisal. Then to my delight Luis began to give the kitten a fulsome tongue-wash. Interestingly, the tiny cat started to respond to Luis' persistent licking by moving his head and body around until he finally struggled to his feet and, watched warily by Luis, not to mention ourselves, tottered over to the water bowl. After a few timid sips he turned and began eating the dried biscuits we'd put down near him. I heaped praise upon Luis for working his cat magic in restoring Max to a semblance of normality and hoped that they would become good companions in time.

Max spent the rest of the day either close to or being carried around by Catherine, on whom he'd become fixated. Although his demeanour had improved somewhat he still indulged in bouts of mewing and whinging. This melancholic behaviour continued over the succeeding weeks and it all proved to unsettle us because we generally maintained a happy household in which our cats are afforded every care and indulgence. We were not accustomed to any of our cats showing a state of such wretchedness as we detected in our new red boy, Max.

Grappling for a solution I spent long hours in the conservatory with Luis for company whilst Catherine ministered to Max. Suddenly, the penny dropped: I knew, without a shadow of a doubt, what was causing Max to suffer those tortured feelings. I should have known earlier from my long experience in clinical psychology. The kitten was suffering from 'Separation Syndrome'. He desperately missed his twin brother. That explained his behaviour at Jane's the day we came to pick him up and it clarified the reasons for his subsequent conduct with us. I recalled my memories of the two tiny mites cuddled together in their box the first time we visited to see Max, and my heart bled with the emotional realization that it was I who had been instrumental in tearing them part when I could very easily at that time have bought them both. Me, who had lectured on the psychology of twins and tutored students at university on the insights culled from research on the subject. I felt ashamed and humbled. Now I would have to find a way to redeem myself and console a little being who had lost the other half of himself through my stupidity. But Max would have nothing to do with me. He cringed whenever I tried to hold him. Perhaps he knew who was to blame and could not forgive me. Cats never forget a wrong done to them.

A call to Jane confirmed my worst feelings. She described how the two kittens had always wanted to be together, with Max avidly searching out his brother if they became separated.

I asked her why she hadn't told me. She explained that she ran a business in which she raised kittens as well as she could, but then she needed to sell them to other cat lovers. To do so she had to mask her own feeling of love for them or else she would end up keeping every one of them herself.

'I understand and do not blame you but what can I do to help Max?'

'Time will heal him, especially with all the love that you and Catherine have for your cats,' she replied.

Meanwhile, back at the cottage we had to deal with the fact that Max not only had lost the comfort and companionship of his little brother but also had been deprived of his safety zone, because it seemed that his twin was the dominant kitten. We made up our minds that we would simply give him as much care and comfort as possible and try to involve him with the other cats as far as plausible. Luis willingly befriended Max and was content to lie with him in the various bed-cushions we provided for our cats but he drew the line at sharing his food bowl with the kitten, who received a few admonitory cuffs around the head for assuming he could eat with Luis. We sympathized with Max, who desperately needed to be close to another cat to fill the gap left by his brother's absence and we watched with compassion as he toddled round the cottage after Luis.

I thought it was also time to introduce him to Pablo but watched apprehensively as the big cat acted very much in the guise of the alpha male. Their first encounter was passably pacific; Pablo sniffed and licked the kitten's head, and then hissed and gently laid his huge paw on Max's head as if to say, 'Know your place and don't bother me!' Max cowered and trembled and didn't move for several moments. When it was over, he began washing himself as cats do when stressed. Then, in what seemed to be a delayed reaction, Max started to tremble and shake uncontrollably. Just as I was about to intervene, Luis, who had been watching, strolled over and lay down alongside Max as if to say by means of his body language: 'Don't worry about it; everything is fine.' It seemed to work because Max stopped shaking, cuddled into Luis and went to sleep, no doubt overcome by his emotions.

When I witnessed this it gave me hope that Max would perhaps soon transfer the attachment he had for his absent brother to Luis. Ever so gradually over the weeks and months that followed this appeared to be what was in fact taking place. Luis, however, remained undeniably the dominant partner, not averse to treating the newcomer to a cuff around the ears now and then to keep him straight. The essence of this relationship admirably suited Luis' lordly pretensions and Max's neurotic needs for comfort and protection. As far as Max was concerned, he was glad to be the follower and seemed to appreciate the developing bond with Luis, and yet his eyes retained an unfailing look of sadness. Only Catherine, with her bountiful show of affection, could put him at ease. Even so, during that first miserable year for him, Max never purred once. I was still very much sidelined by all that was going on with Max because he would have nothing to do with me. His rejection of me was most upsetting but nothing I did made an impression on him. No cat had ever failed to respond to my overtures of friendship like Max had.

Just when I thought that Max was improving we both noticed that he was beginning to lose his fur. The condition had probably been deteriorating for some time but it became unmistakable and we realized that there was something seriously wrong with him. We tried changing his diet to see if richer food would help him. To this end I bought him oily fish such as fresh mackerel and salmon, but to no avail. Then we spotted a number of little sores on his bare patches which could only be insect bites, though Max did not have any fleas on him. He fast began to assume the appearance of the proverbial scabby cat. We tried treating him with all kinds of home remedies, which included skin creams and saline sprays, but nothing seemed to work.

We hesitated about taking him to a vet because Max went into a paroxysm of terror if a stranger appeared anywhere near him, as we discovered when we enlisted the help of workmen for odd jobs around the house or garden. He possessed that haunted look of apprehension which meant that he was in a perpetual state of readiness to be alarmed. The sudden noise of heavy traffic, low-flying jet aircraft or knocks on the door would send him into such a traumatic state that he would hide away for hours until all was clear. Even if we moved suddenly or dropped something in the kitchen or exclaimed loudly it would send him into such a spooked state that he would crawl, bellyflop style, along the floor to escape. Perhaps the state of health he was suffering, I thought, was similar to humans suffering from alopecia (hair loss) due to nervous conditions.

After conferring with Catherine I rang the vet and described the condition Max was suffering. I told him that I wanted him to make a house call since our cat was too nervous for a visit to the clinic. He then advised me that if the cat was suffering so badly it might be sensible to 'have him put down to relieve his suffering'. I told him that it was out of the question and arranged for him to come the following day at 11 a.m.

The vet duly arrived with all his veterinary paraphernalia and examined Max, who was clutched tightly in Catherine's arms. After using his stethoscope he pronounced that Max's heartbeat was four times the norm, which I could see plainly enough from looking at one of his legs which was shaking wildly and thumping against Catherine's lap like a drumbeat. He said, 'I will give him an injection of antibiotics and another of steroids but if he shows no improvement after one week then my original suggestion to you stands because his immune system may be too poor to enable him to recover either from his physical allergic reaction to the bites, psychological condition of nervous response or both.'

Max closed his eyes and slumped against Catherine as the injections were administered.

Poor Max, I thought, after the vet had left and Max was once more curled as if in a coma in his bed-cushion. I posed the question to myself: 'Is he too vulnerable to survive in this tough world?'

He did not stir all that evening, not even when we stroked him and brought food in for him. Ultimately, we retired to bed, half afraid that he would die in his sleep. But a remarkable development occurred in the days that followed his treatment. Max began to improve. The changes were minute at first; then we began to detect fur growing on his body where formerly there had been a bald patch. He seemed calmer and developed a healthy appetite. After two weeks the changes were phenomenal in comparison to how he had been. He was still easily scared but his reactions were less extreme. The sores on his skin were beginning to fade and we decided to order another treatment session for him. This time a young lady vet visited and took an instant liking to Max. She fussed him and spoke soothingly to him as she administered the injections so expertly that Max hardly trembled. We were very impressed. She told us over a cup of tea that she specialized in clinical treatments for small animals, mainly pets, and that for her it was a childhood dream come true. On her advice we booked one further treatment in a fortnight.

After the completion of this course of treatment Max was like a new cat. No doubt the antibiotics had restored his skin to health but also the steroids had induced a placid effect to his manner and disposition. The medicines had 'done him the world of good', as my grandmother would often pronounce after seeing someone changed for the better.

Max continued to avoid me but was more responsive with Catherine and would spend hours on her lap in the evening or, if she stretched out on the sofa or by the fireside, he would lie alongside her. One morning at breakfast time he jumped onto her lap and as she stroked him Max began to purr loudly. It was the first of many such events. And so Max grew to be more firmly encompassed in our hearts and any thoughts of putting him down were summarily dismissed. To my mind this was unthinkable but I understood that the vet had made the suggestion out of professional consideration of our cat.

To his credit Max was growing into a most handsome cat, with a thick matt of vibrant red fur covering his head and back, which was given a vivid contrast by the pure white fur of his chest and paws. His tail was a magnificent upright long crimson plume of fine hair. And Max's eyes, deep golden gems, had lost the haunted look and they expressed devoted love to my wife Catherine. Following his own agenda and dispositions he would only sit on her lap and it was her alone he favoured with his purrs and from whom he accepted strokes.

I began to realize that for his own protection Max had made a deal with himself about the way he would relate to the world in which he found himself, and to preserve his independence he would restrict his trust and his self to Catherine and Luis exclusively. I understood the psychology of his riven emotions but felt hurt at being rejected. I hoped that in the future he would also accept me as a friend, though he most certainly was making me wait a long time for it.

Reflecting on the time when Jane rang to tell me that the red kitten had arrived, I remembered that I had been filled with excitement and when we first visited him I recalled that I had been the stranger who had plucked him out of his cosy box away from his little brother. I pictured in my mind's eye how the twin kittens had been cuddled into each other as if glued together. When I'd lifted him out, I now recollected, he had cried piteously at being parted from his brother. Perhaps from the time of that experience he had associated my scent and the sound of my voice with being parted from his twin and blamed me for the later separation.

It took a long while before he was ready to forgive and forget. It was only after two years that he began to give me some limited recognition for all my efforts to make friends. The curious, if not hilarious, thing about the whole affair was that Catherine had bought Max for me as a belated Christmas present.

It is an undeniable fact that nothing lasts forever, even the frame of mind of a large red and white cat called Max. The change happened one winter's evening as I sat alone in the sitting room reading a book. As I shifted around in my seat I realized that I had an empty paper packet in my pocket that I had meant to dispose of in the kitchen trash can. Taking it out I began absentmindedly to scrunch it in my free hand whilst reading. Suddenly, I heard a meow and on looking around I saw Max nearby giving me a fixed stare. Just then Catherine came into the room and, quickly grasping the situation, she said, 'He wants you to throw the paper ball for him.'

I looked again at Max, who was paying rapt attention to me

and at the rounded piece of paper in my hand, and understood what she meant, but I was still amazed when, as I tossed the paper to a far corner of the room, Max whirled and raced after it. He then picked it up in his mouth and jogged back towards me to drop the missive at my feet. Then he looked at me expectantly. That glance meant only one thing: 'Throw it for me again. I want to play.'

Catherine and I laughed. Max was showing us another facet of his personality; he knew how to retrieve. I was so elated at this development that I discarded my book and continued the game with Max. We must have played for nearly an hour, until we were both tired, and he lay down exhausted on the fireside rug. This welcome sign that he was at last ready and willing to relate to me both astonished me and pleased me immensely. I was reminded of Carlos and how he loved to retrieve and would initiate the playtime by carrying his cloth toy mice to me to be thrown; he was such a fun-loving cat and I still missed him sorely.

I began now to have high hopes that Max would take over this role so that we could enter into a new phase of having fun together that would build a friendship bond between us. The mechanism of our new game-playing took on a daily rhythm of its own: throw . . . run . . . catch . . . retrieve . . . return. As Max slowly began to acknowledge my part in his life as non-threatening, I was aware that he remained cautious if not jittery whenever I happened to enter his space and if I moved too quickly he would scoot away. But he was now, more often than not, ever ready to play 'Retrieve Ball'. It was clear that Max had chosen this method of relating to me as a way of breaking the ice and in due course other changes to our relationship began to emerge, but only in Max's good time. Luis looked on these games of mine with Max with a mild blandness which precluded his own involvement. Luis never did learn to retrieve. I expect he considered it beneath his dignity.

The way that Max's personality has developed is epitomized by the manner in which he plays. He developed a love of playing with his toy mouse. He has a large one, which I bought for him, that is his favourite, possibly because it squeaks when he bites it and tosses it around as cats do. If Max is in the mood he will hunt out this toy and perform acrobatic manoeuvres which defy gravity. He engages in leaps, mid-air turns and catches that leave him lying stretched out and panting for breath. Then he revives and the play continues a while longer. When the mouse is grasped in his mouth he makes a quick twist of his head and hurls the toy high in the air and then runs to make the catch, pouncing on it and batting it around with deft slaps of his paws until he is once more tired out and must succumb to a brief catnap, slumped in his cushion-bed. But this play activity is conditional upon it being solely for his own private enjoyment. He will not tolerate interference. If one of the other cats attempts to join in, Max ceases his play, looks upset and retreats somewhere to sulk.

Such behaviour from Max calls to mind a story that one of

the readers of *Paw Tracks in the Moonlight* related to me over the telephone when she was telling me about her Maine Coon cats. She also lives in a rural area and has a large garden. One day she caught sight of her cat called Barnaby playing indoors with a live mouse which he'd brought from the garden. Not wanting any rodents in the house she removed it and set it free outside, only to find that Barnaby had managed to slip out and once again returned with the mouse.

'No Barnaby,' she said. 'You cannot have a pet mouse!'

But despite her actions, removing the mouse several times, Barnaby persisted in finding and retrieving it to play with in the house. He obviously wanted the mouse as a playmate because he never bit it or hurt it in any way as far as she could see. Eventually the situation took a radically different turn when Claudius, the alpha male of her cats, strolled in and spotted Barnaby playing with the mouse. Without a moment's hesitation Claudius swiftly seized the mouse and with a single shake of his jaws killed it. Then with the mouse in his mouth he slowly walked over to the now distraught Barnaby, dropped the dead mouse in front of him and glared at him as if to say: 'Remember that you are a cat. Cats kill mice, OK, get it?'

My caller went on to tell me that Barnaby's response was to gently touch the corpse with his paw, all the while making whimpering cries over the dead body of the mouse he'd wanted as a friend. She said that if a cat could cry then Barnaby wept.

From my reading of the kind of cat that Max is, I believe him to be much like Barnaby because he has such a gentle and fragile disposition. This in so many ways renders him vulnerable and afraid of the world at large. He is moulded like those everywhere who suffer desperately with serious nervous conditions which make them much more sensitive to the feelings of others. Max is an extremely sensitive cat who wears his emotions very clearly on the outside for all to see.

Another aspect of Max's character is his intelligence in finding solutions to problems. On one of our infrequent trips with the cats to the local cattery so that we could take a short holiday, Max revealed a clever ruse to get himself back home again. When we arrive at the cattery we always take the time to introduce the cats to the environment they will be sharing and the people who will be caring for them whilst we are away. We try to make the experience as non-stressful as possible for our pets. On this occasion Pablo and Luis, ever the confident and self-assured ones, made a quick tour of inspection of the compound and settled on high wooden platforms from which they could survey the area without undue difficulty, especially the compounds housing other cats. Max timidly looked around, sniffed the floor and then disappeared. I thought he'd gone inside to hide in one of the beds. As we said our goodbyes we each carried a cat box back to the car but I noticed that Catherine was lagging behind me and having some difficulty carrying her one, which appeared to be lopsided.

'I don't know what's wrong with this,' she said. 'It's so awkward to carry and it feels heavy.'

I took the box from her and checked to see if there was

something wrong with the handle which was making it become lopsided, but the handle was fine. Then I opened the grill door at the front of the box and imagine my utter astonishment at seeing Max clinging to the back of the box with his claws fastened in the air inlets. He had made up his mind that the cattery was not for him and worked out that if he could stow away in the box that brought him he could return home but he needed to hide so that we wouldn't detect him. We burst out laughing at the sheer ingenuity of his escape plan, which mirrored some Second World War escape efforts, especially the one involving a 'Wooden Horse', of Allies held in German prisoner of war camps. We brought him out, congratulated him and Catherine gave him a surfeit of hugs. I saw that she was crying a little at her red cat's cleverness in arranging to get back home. Much to his dismay, and it took us extra time to settle him, we took him back to his apartment to rejoin Pablo and Luis. We then told them all again that we would soon be back. Hurrying away to the car we felt very guilty at leaving them even though we knew they would be very well looked after.

As I mentioned earlier, whenever we return from a holiday break we are not greeted with abundant friendliness by our cats when we fetch them back from the cattery. Our cats are enormously sensitive, some would say spoilt, and like their brethren worldwide are capable of sulking when events go contrary to their expectation and liking. This behaviour is meant to punish us for leaving them and it takes a while to thaw out. This time when we came back, following the escape ploy by Max, we were in receipt not only of the customary huffiness by our cats but also by a message that provoked extreme anxiety. The cattery manager informed us that Pablo had needed to be taken to the vet's because of an angry-looking sore on his right front paw. When we examined him at home we saw an ugly red blob between the toes of the paw. On contacting the surgery in Alnwick we were further alarmed by the prognosis that it was a tumour which required immediate surgery. An appointment was made in all haste and Pablo duly had an operation that necessitated the amputation of two toes in order to excise the growth, which was diagnosed as a 'spindle cell tumour'.

We brought him home with relief that it was all over but we were warned that it could recur. When he'd recovered from the anaesthetic he demonstrated just what a tough guy he was by wrenching free from the tight-fitting bandage which encased his leg and angrily demanding, as only cats can demand by means of piteous, hollow-sounding wails, to be allowed out. I opened the door for him, thinking that he would probably just want to sit outside on the patio to prove to himself that he was free again after all he'd endured. However, he proceeded to climb one of the highest trees in the garden and I could just make out his dark form resting inside the leafy foliage midway up. He stayed there for three hours before coming down to have his dinner.

Apart from hobbling slightly he appeared his old self and didn't even react when the two other cats spat at him because of the chemical smell on his fur. Later, they seemed to relent and, as he lay relaxed after his meal, they set to and gave him a jolly good tongue-wash. But both Max and Luis kept slavering and shaking their heads at the unnatural taste.

We pampered Pablo over the next few weeks to help to restore him to full health and hoped that he would make a full recovery without any recurrence of the problem. Meanwhile, we were enjoying a period of warm sunny weather and we took every opportunity to sit out in the garden and to bask in the glory that sunlight renders on the most ordinary landscapes. In our case we already have a beautiful garden but the sunshine makes it even more so. At evening time, for several days, the sunsets lit up the whole cloudless sky and made an eye-catching display of dazzling bands of red, orange, green and turquoise colours. During this spell we were pleased to see Pablo wandering less and spending more time with us.

Luis and Max were taken out separately from the compound and, wearing harnesses, were led around the garden for investigative walks. In truth, neither of them walks in the normal sense of the word. Luis likes to travel in accelerated spurts from one interesting area to another. He will stop and have a real good sniff at a bush or flower and then make a further spurt which would almost drag me off my feet. Then he might climb and claw his way up a tree, only to become entangled by his lead as he explores the branches. I have to go and get a stepladder to undo the muddle and coax him to come down, which is when I usually find my cat is at his most disobedient. Catherine has often found similar difficulties at times when she leads Max around. Max does not walk; he parades, delicately splaying his large paws in a stately fashion. He slowly proceeds with his head held high and his fluffy orange-red tail held aloft behind him like a banner. While on the whole it can be said that Max has the sweetest disposition, especially when he is in Catherine's company, he can also evince an intransigent attitude at times.

I remember one time when he was out in the garden being led along the paths and, as he meandered around the shrubs and trees, a slight difference of opinion occurred between him and Catherine with regard to the direction the saunter should take. Normally Max would be most amenable but on this occasion the situation developed into a full-blown dispute as Max dug his snowy white paws in the lawn and stubbornly refused to budge. Catherine was equally adamant, not wishing to have her clothes ensnared by rose thorns. The end result was that Max lost his temper and began furiously hissing. Having watched this pantomime with amusement from my vantage point in the greenhouse, I decided to intervene and to the surprise of both parties I strode out and picked up Max, divested him of his harness and lead and placed him in the compound. He set up an apologetic wailing intended to make Catherine come to his rescue but by this time she had had enough and left him to muse on his sorrows and reflect on his naughty behaviour. Later that afternoon Max showed in his attitude to both of us that he was thoroughly miffed over the incident, though when supper time came around, and Pablo and Luis were served their biscuits, Max began reviewing the cost his sulk was causing him and concluded that it was better to overlook the episode so that he could enjoy an evening snack.

Trying never to sleep on an argument was a maxim we tended to foster at Owl Cottag. Thus we made sufficient fuss of Max to yet again ease the troubled mind of our temperamental rouge cat and all calm and peace was restored to the happy home. Since it had been such a fine day, with clear skies, the stars shone down in all their splendour that night and I stayed late in the conservatory to view their brilliance in the company of Luis on my right side and Max on my left. Pablo, as was his wont, was out on the prowl. We saw no owls but spotted two red squirrels relishing a good meal at the peanut-feeders we hang for the songbirds. I left the room for bed, sonorously serenaded goodnight by the soft snores of my two boy cats.

Max is a remarkable cat, as I increasingly recognize now that I have been allowed to share his company more closely. It has taken fully two years for him to change his mind towards me and permit me to be his friend. He now competes with Luis for my attention and strokes. This sometimes causes trouble. Occasionally, Luis takes offence when he sees Max sitting anywhere near me for a head rub and caress, and then he will bully Max into a hasty withdrawal by growling and cuffing him across the face. Even though he is smaller than Max he can act the thug at times and he is especially possessive of me and my affections. I believe this attitude stems from his notion that he is personally descended from an elite line of royal cats who are superior to all other forms of life, including humans. Cats can display a remnant of the attitude of the Ancient Egyptian cat-gods, accounting for some of them to be viewed as snooty, aloof and even hostile.

But to return to Max: he is charm personified, at least most of the time. This genial feature of his character is revealed not only in his need for affection and harmony in his life but also because he wants opportunities to play. I have already mentioned his ability to retrieve objects thrown for him as part of a game plan that is all his own, which he will happily pursue until he is exhausted. Further to this he will, when he is in the mood, seek out a toy of some sort. He also likes to dance. This is an activity he indulges by himself, for himself alone. In some respects this dance game could be described as akin to the antics of a whirling dervish in that he runs and jumps around whilst turning circles, coils himself into the form of a spring, and erupts into a gigantic leap, wherein he twists and flays the air with his paws. On landing he gallops off at express speed, upstairs and downstairs, and ends with a bound onto the top of some furniture. Dance finished, he will assiduously wash himself all over with his tongue. To witness this performance is to be enthralled and at the same time concerned for his safety, not to mention that of the furnishings. To date nothing has been broken, only scratched. If Carlos could have seen Max dance, I'm certain he would have launched himself wholeheartedly into joining him.

This amazing feat of creative gymnastics, or letting off steam, is not discharged regularly but it would appear to await the spur of an aesthetic impulse within Max. Whenever it happens the other cats are mystified, if not a little apprehensive. When we are privileged to view it we find it most entertaining and applaud heartily and loudly cheer him. This dance of his expresses what is singularly Max, much different from when he first came to us. At times he even displays a positively sanguine attitude to life and the universe.

One day Max discovered he had a taste for venison sausage. It happened one morning when, after a heavy bout of writing, I was relaxing in front of the television and Catherine brought me a plate of grilled sausage cut into small sections. Suddenly Max appeared at my side, licking his lips.

'You won't like any of this, Max,' I said, knowing that he had a fussy taste which I didn't believe would extend to venison and sage. But when he saw me enjoying the treat he leaned up and planted his two paws on my knee.

'All right, but I hope it doesn't make you sick,' I warned him.

Never doubt a cat's propensity to have what it wants. No sooner had I offered him a morsel of sausage than it was gone in a trice.

'Well, I would never have believed it if I hadn't seen it,' I said to no one in particular.

Thereafter, Max proceeded to eat several more pieces, relishing the taste with a purring accompaniment. Meanwhile, Luis wandered in, sniffed the piece I felt obliged to offer him and walked away in disgust. Pablo also gave it a cursory inspection but would not deign to eat it. I made a mental note to organize a trip to the rural market town of Rothbury and visit the self-styled 'Best Butcher in the World' housed at the foot of the main street. I would buy a supply of venison and sage sausage for Max and for me. Max and I were fast building a friendship bonded not only from playing games of retrieve but also by sharing the same taste in sausages. Whatever next? I thought. Aren't cats mysterious and marvellous to know?

We were about to go through a very difficult period at Owl Cottage, as the few thoughts I wrote down at the time reveal:

Bad news! Pablo has developed another tumour on his right foot. And so we have had again the collective trauma for our precious little family of having to subject Pablo once more to the surgeon's knife. He has come back this time with even less toes on the afflicted foot. The other two cats are seeking in their various ways, usually by licking his head and lying near to him, to show their concern and sympathy, whilst he is making the most of his life by still trying to act the big tough guy. Catherine and I are deeply troubled at what is happening to him.

Meanwhile, I am continuing to write this sequel to *Paw Tracks in the Moonlight*, spurred forward by a host of letters from my readers urging me to write the next book. I work at my laptop at my desk, adjacent to an upstairs window. I am still often visited by Luis, who has learned to sit and lie on his special bed- cushion on the window sill next to me so that I don't have to protect my keyboard from his intrusive paws. Luis may be my more frequent writing partner, but recently Max has shown that he will not be left out and demands his turn at my side. As I write this he is languishing on the window sill, making chittering noises at the birds flying around outside. Now and then he turns his golden eyes on me and I tell him that I am writing about him and all his doings. He yawns and rests his head between paws that are as white as snow and watches me intently until the rhythm of my typing mesmerizes him, and with a soft sigh he catnaps the afternoon away.

The problems with Pablo's paw have become worse and he has had to have the first three inches of his right paw surgically removed. He now really has to hobble around and my heart aches for him, knowing how much he misses his wild wanderings. He spends a lot of his time now in the company of the other cats as if he needs their fellowship in order to come to terms with what is happening to him. He responds joyfully to me when I spend time with him but I am deeply worried about the consequences of these tumours for him. The chief vet cannot help us regarding the reasons for these infections or how to treat them, except for surgical removal. It is frustrating for me to feel the impotency of not knowing what to do to help my beloved cat. He looks at me sad-eyed and I despair at the possibility of losing him.

The end came sooner than expected. Pablo was spending the night with the others in the conservatory, sleeping in his large cushion-bed. Sometime in the middle of the night I was awakened by a cat crying loudly. I hurried downstairs to find both Luis and Max grouped around Pablo, greatly concerned because he was faintly moaning. It was Luis who had cried and awakened me. I tried to reassure them not to worry even though I was worried sick myself. With Catherine's help I lifted Pablo onto a blanket we laid on the table for him. I could tell he was hurting so I crushed a paracetamol tablet in a spoon and mixed it with cod liver oil. Then, while Catherine held him, I managed to get most of it down his mouth. He seemed weaker than I expected and it shocked me to realize that our big loveable Pablo was suffering some serious pain.

We lit the fire and nursed him between us for the rest of the night, all thoughts of bed abandoned. In our anxiety we drank lots of cups of tea, kept Pablo warm and as comfortable as we could, and waited for the morning. Meanwhile, Max and Luis whined and wailed at the sitting-room door so we let them in. I was moved at the solicitude they were showing for Pablo as they insisted on being near him. The signals they were giving me would be a revelation to anyone in the strictly scientific world who regards any creature below themselves on the species scale as a dumb animal. Luis and Max were desperately trying to console and care for Pablo in his hour of need. After all, it was Luis who had alerted me to his condition.

As soon as we could we took Pablo to an emergency clinic and were told what we suspected and dreaded. The condition causing the tumours had spread to infect his whole body and his state of health was terminal; he was also suffering acute pain as his vitals deteriorated. At this forecast Catherine burst into tears and simply hugged Pablo. I gestured with a movement of my head for the vet to come into the corridor for a quiet word.

'I understand what you have told me but I beg of you to consider relieving his pain sufficiently so that we can spend a last day with him before you put him away. Can you do that?'

He replied, 'I should terminate him now to release him from his suffering and I'm not sure I can manage to do the alleviation of pain you want.'

'But you can try, can't you?' I burst out.

His face flushed red and he looked away from me. Then he turned and faced me with an icy stare. 'I'll do my professional best but you must bring him back in twenty-four hours, for his sake.'

I nodded assent and joined Catherine. We drove back home with heavy hearts and a heavily sedated Pablo. We spent the evening huddled together with our three cats, watching television and not watching at the same time. Luis and Max sensed that something final had been concluded and Luis in particular kept looking my way and making muted questioning cries. The following morning neither Catherine nor I could eat breakfast and made do with coffee. Pablo showed no inclination to eat but seemed surprisingly buoyant.

'It's the steroids keeping him comfortable,' I said to Catherine's questioning glances. We made him comfortable on a bed-cushion on the table between us and Pablo purred the morning away as we stroked and talked lovingly to him. Shadows of the last moments of Toby Jug's life came back as a kind of nightmarish déjà vu as we put Pablo in his box for his last journey to the vet's.

It was over very quickly and dealt with in a most clinically professional way, but we were in an emotional turmoil at the demise of our first Maine Coon Boy and we were very close to tears. The male vet and the nurse gently positioned Pablo on the bench. The vet took hold of his left paw began to inject an overdose of powerful anaesthetic into his bloodstream. Instantly, Pablo realized that he was dying and reared up out of the grasp of the young nurse. Urgently, I reached across and held his head to steady him just as the injection began to overwhelm him.

He then did a remarkable thing. He turned that big head I loved so much and looked directly at me: his eyes said goodbye to me. Then they clouded over and he slumped to the table and was gone. I hastened out from the clinic unashamedly in floods of tears. Catherine joined me in the car, equally distraught. On the way home she said the sensible thing.

'Remember we still have two other boys who need us and for their sake we need to act normal.'

I nodded and wondered how many times I could survive a broken heart. We didn't bury Pablo's body at the cottage. We had him cremated because I feared that whatever virulent virus had killed him might contaminate the soil and infect Luis and Max.

The night after the death of Pablo, I sat in the darkness of the conservatory and wondered how Pablo had become infected with what turned out to be such a deadly virus. Veterinary science could not offer an explanation and my thoughts were purely speculative. But I did wonder if Pablo's predilection for eating rabbits he caught on his hunting trips could have been a factor in his demise, especially since he seemed to like to eat the brains of his kills. I remembered the lethal virus myxomatosis, which was a manmade neural agent that accounted for mass destruction of the rabbit population in the 1950s. I wondered if some remnant had remained in the surviving rabbit population and had infected Pablo.

I missed him terribly and carved his name into the trunk of one of the trees he habitually climbed. I would never forget him. His photograph, mounted on the window sill in our bedroom, haunts me each morning as I open the bedroom window for air. He was magnificent. Catherine and I both loved him dearly. I never find it easy to say goodbye to a cherished and much loved animal friend.

It is some weeks since I wrote the above and during that time Max has matured to an astonishing extent. I find that now his behaviour is full of surprises. It just goes to show, I reflect, that cats, especially Maine Coons, are creatures of infinite depth and spread of personality. He has, to all intents and purposes, become a calmer, more affable and less troubled cat than he was. Also, he has become a true friend of mine and I feel most privileged at the welcome change in his attitude to me. The experience has taught me that one can never assume the love of an animal, especially a cat. One needs to earn it, to merit it.

When Max is taken for a walk around our large garden he parades slowly as if he is savouring every moment of the experience. He meanders here and there seemingly at random but I suspect he has his own agenda. He always inspects the barbeque and the bags of garden waste for any mysterious smells, he rubs his nose and head in the petals of any flowers he comes across in his path, just as Luis does, and he appears to delight in having a climb up any tree that takes his fancy. All of this is accomplished in an unhurried manner and he obviously enjoys it in a way that quite belies his former nervous rush down the garden to gain refuge in the sanctuary of the conservatory.

When I try to account for the difference in him I can only think that the tranquil ambience of the life we lead in the cottage has affected a change in how he identifies himself in relation to us and the world around him. I also believe that when he was treated with steroids a physical change was induced which allowed a change in his mental attitude. These reasons are speculative but something changed for the better, even if we cannot be sure what it was precisely. It could also be that he was able to change himself by an internal process of self awareness. Cats, like other mammals, are sentient beings and Maine Coons are reputed to be the most intelligent of all cats. In this respect I have observed Max behaving in a fashion very similar to Toby Jug's thoughtful pre-occupation with his own mental processes and feelings. I am aware that Max, in common with the other Maine Coon cats we have had, takes time out to have a think and I see him on the scratching post pedestal, especially in the moonlight, reflecting on life and the world as he sees it from a cat's perspective. At such times he is impervious to me, even though I am following a similar line of thought from a human perspective. If I then call to him when he is in this mode he doesn't respond because I am interrupting his mental flow. Sometime later, perhaps five or ten minutes after I have called to him, he will come to me with a friendly cry as if to say, 'What was it you wanted?' I will say, 'I understand, Max,' and he will then give me a throaty purr because we now comprehend each other. It is just like it was with Toby Jug. We are totally simpatico with each other. We often spend hours this way in the comfort of the conservatory, winter and summer alike.

There are also occasions when he comes looking to find me. Once discovered I am treated to a non-verbal display of curved back, upright and wavering tail, face-rubbing affection and stroking against the side of my chair or the lower length of my leg. This means in cat language: 'Hello. I've not forgotten about you and just wanted to keep in friendly touch.'

Such a demonstration of affection merits a stream of soothing and prizing words and strokes from me, after which, satisfied that our fellowship is in a good state, he will trot off to some other concern of his like having a game of chase upstairs and downstairs with Luis.

'Welcome to the world of free agents,' is my frequent plaudit to him as I congratulate him on his new found maturity. Now, whenever I settle down in the evening, Max comes to lie next to me, or as near as Luis will allow him since he usually takes pride of place on my left-hand side. If Luis challenges him, Max retreats for succour with Catherine and, if she is stretching out on the sofa, he will drape his not inconsiderable size over her like a warm blanket.

To my understanding, the way that Max has come to show love and affection for me after several years of ignoring me totally is nothing short of a phenomenon and leads me to realize that cats have profound and often latent attributes of personality which, as in Max's case, only truly emerge when the cat feels particularly secure in the love of those who care for him. It makes me wonder to see the astonishment which some of our friends show at the close bonds we have with our cats. They express views, which are not uncommon, such as: 'But cats are generally very self-focused animals and independent creatures, but yours are so different.'

I tell them that I believe that any animal, be it a horse, dog, cat, parrot or budgerigar, will always respond to kindly attention and caring affection, and that I know this because I've made good friendships with them all.

But to return to how I am with our cats, I can honestly state that quite apart from loving them deeply and being loved in return, I know them inside their minds and they know me; we are linked on a mental plane of mutual affection and understanding. They have even responded to my growing love of music, especially classical. One night as I was watching *Amadeus*, the story of Mozart's life, I was troubled to hear a discordant, rumbling interference to the soundtrack. I tried to find out where it was coming from until I realized that Max, who was lying behind me, was singing his purrs to accompany a piano concerto in the film. I was humbled by the discovery. Since then, we have found that Max is very fond of music and it was a revelation to both Catherine and myself to find that one of his favourite recordings is the soundtrack from the film *South Pacific*. Who can deny therefore that cats not only have mindful awareness and intuitive intelligence but also that they possess aesthetic appreciation of the creative arts? I often share appreciation of a beautiful sunset with my cats, in the same way that I did with Toby Jug and Fynn the horse on our camping trek into the Cheviot Hills one summer, some long years ago.

Max has now fully lived up to and deservedly earned the name that Jane mistakenly wrote out on his pedigree certificate: Maxamillion. He is truly one in a million.

ENDINGS

I am now near to closing this saga of our life at Owl Cottage with our four Maine Coon cats. But first of all let me backtrack to the beginning to illustrate how we changed the cottage to become the very special Owl Cottage it is today. When Catherine and I first arrived, after newly acquiring the cottage and before we had any cats, we were faced with a place which had been severely neglected and which needed much repair and renovation. There were two stone outhouses which had become dilapidated with age and were now falling apart. I remembered them from my earlier time and had used them then as storage areas. One had also provided a shelter for Toby Jug in case of bad weather when I was not at home. We had these demolished and the stone was used again to build some low decorative garden walls. The residue was used with newer stone to build a garage, since the old wooden one was a ruin.

Further up the garden on the left-hand side, there used to be an unsightly horse paddock with a powdered grit base, partially surrounded by concrete. We dug it all up and, with the aid of several loads of topsoil, we were able to grass the patch once more and plant trees, lots and lots of trees, enough to turn the whole site into a woodland glade. Then we dug borders for flowering shrubs and flowers.

Next we turned our attention to renovating the inside of the cottage. A new bathroom and kitchen were fitted and given stone-tiled floors, while the old, ramshackle conservatory was replaced with a larger annexe, with wooden flooring, double-glazed windows and a glass door. We stripped the thick wallpaper from the room between the bathroom and the kitchen and installed a wood-burning stove within the arched fireplace. This is the living space we refer to as the cosy room. Painting and decorating followed until the look of the interior of the cottage was renewed and suited our taste.

It was at this stage that we recognized that the cottage would not be a home without a cat. Pablo came and took possession of us, the cottage and especially the garden, followed in fairly quick succession by those three other Maine Coon cats called Carlos, Luis and Max.

If I take an imaginary stroll down memory lane I become aware that the garden has figured as centre stage to our time at the cottage and has been the medium through which Catherine and I, and our family of cats, have lived our lives. Each tree, each bush and each flower is known personally to me and in turn to each of our cats.

In my younger life here at Owl Cottage my cat Toby Jug was fond of taking me on a tour of the garden to show me, for example, where the hedgehog hid during daylight, where a field mouse had built a nest of dried grasses in the compost heap which was now abandoned and where the grey toad had hibernated in a dank crevice formed by two ill-fitting stones.

These places are still there for the most part, but sadly Toby Jug is not. Yet I have found that my new cats have taken over this practice and on our walks around the garden they are anxious to point out to me the secret places they have discovered.

I will always revere the old gnarled apple tree with branches of thick rough bark which Toby Jug loved to climb and under which he is buried. Further up the garden there is a tall, green beech tree which bears the claw marks of Pablo's climbs. On his death his name was carved on its trunk by me and beneath the leaves of its branches his ashes were scattered to remind the earth that he, too, was once here. The trees growing in the compound we had built to house and protect our cats, with its runways and platforms, provide excellent shelter from stormy weather and also shade from the sun. If he is not relaxing in his hutch, Luis likes to hide in the thick stems of bamboo in readiness to ambush any hapless bird that might squeeze through the gaps in the chicken wire fencing; Max prefers, on fine days anyway, to settle high up in the canopy of the lilac tree. At ground level there is a flourishing rosebush, the white and pink flecked petals of which, when blown by the summer wind, may drop to adorn a flat grey stone, streaked with silver, that covers the grave of a prince of derring-do. On Midsummer's Eve, when wood nymphs, if such there be, are abroad and one chances by this stone, it might whisper the name Carlos in deference to the spirit of a fallen hero.

In a late autumn afternoon when I'm sitting at the top of the garden I'm sure to catch a glimpse of at least one bushy-tailed thief gathering a harvest from the branches of the hazelnut tree.

A stray sunbeam identifies the culprit as the red squirrel which lives with its mate in the plantation across the road. Gone now are the charming flowers of spring but the brief dalliance of white snowdrops, yellow and purple crocuses and golden daffodils remain painted on the backdrop of my memory. Summertime brings the brilliance of tulips from the vivid scarlet of 'Apeldoorn' to the vibrant yellow of 'Bellona' and the creamy white and green tints of 'Spring Green'. Then the season moves on to present us with the delectable sights and scents of the tea rose garden that Catherine and I hold most dear.

Here and there in our garden areas we have often found a single flower which is out of place, and we were at first mystified as to how this plant, be it daffodil or tulip or hyacinth, could have come to be planted where there are no others of its kind. One day in the local cafe at Felton we were remarking on this strange phenomenon when an experienced gardener enlightened us. From his account, which I have no reason to doubt, the phantom planters are field mice which dig up some flower bulbs in autumn and replant them elsewhere as an emergency food store for winter. If the mouse forgets about them, or more likely perishes, then the bulbs will flower in the spring in their new setting. In this way, just as one example, the wildlife contributes to the natural beauty of our garden. I have even seen a coal tit planting sunflower seeds that I have put out for the birds to eat in container pots. Like the field mouse, he is helping with the gardening and nature is spreading and renewing herself with the help of her wild creatures.

There is also an abundance of small conifers and bushes in the flowering borders, which create dense and inviting areas of thick foliage for our two remaining boy cats, Luis and Max, to explore as they romp around the garden with us holding their leads. It is their practice to plunge their heads deeply inside some of the bushes they encounter, looking for birds and mice, but when this occurs in contact with a shrub called Choisya or Mexican Orange Blossom, as it is better known, the pollen from its star-shaped scented flowers causes an explosive fit of cat sneezes.

In Northumberland, autumnal fogs and drizzling mists are to be expected but this is also the time when hibernating animals need to stock up body fat to tide them through the winter. From my vantage point in the conservatory, my cats and I share a window on the world of the garden outside. We sit in complete darkness with the blinds open and we watch in silence. My cats, especially dear Pablo, taught me the cat skill of silent watchfulness. So we listen and observe. Our eyes cannot penetrate the misty curtains stretched before us outside until, that is, a pale moon illuminates white veils of a hazy vapour cloud. Then the boy cats and I lean forward excitedly as dark shadowy shapes can be seen secretly foraging over the grass for slugs, worms and snails. The moon brightens and casts a silvery translucent shroud over the dank foliage of bushes and trees, and suddenly we hear the muted scream of a little owl on the hunt. Then we dimly recognize a resident family of hedgehogs, a female and three piglets moving searchingly between the darkened trunks of trees. We watch in awe as this panoply of nature unfolds delightfully before us.

There is one exceptional feature of life at Owl Cottage which I must mention and that is the bountiful bird life which inhabits and visits our garden. During Pablo's time here I had to be cautious about attracting songbirds by hanging feeders out because he was an accomplished killer of wildlife; it was his instinctive drive, but since his departure I feel free to encourage birdlife to nest and raise their families in our garden. To this end I have placed bird boxes on the more mature trees, and on the wall to the left of the conservatory, where there is a heavy growth of greenery, I have inserted nesting boxes to encourage sparrows, titmice, wrens and finches to nest and raise their young.

Meanwhile, I make sure that the bird-feed station around the bird table is well supplied with sunflower seeds and dried worms, not to mention peanuts. During the day we are regaled by the sight through the conservatory window of goldfinches, nuthatches and great spotted woodpeckers availing themselves of the handouts freely given. Our resident pair of ring doves keeps us amused and enchanted each day by their obvious devotion to each other; they even drink from the bird bath together.

Now that I have almost reached the end of my tale of two people and four Maine Coon cats at Owl Cottage, I am suffering a state of denial about closing this account because it constitutes an ending of what I most treasure in my life. Yet I recognize that

Owl Cottage will always be here for future generations to enjoy and we still have two healthy and extremely happy Maine Coons who, beside their loving attachment to us, have the freedom to savour separate and sentient lives of their own and all that personally matters to them.

I yearn for what was and cannot be again, at least not for me. I know that there are still remote grassy meadows in the woods below the Cheviot Hills where skylarks nest and ascend to sing their throbbing hymns to life; I have been there and I have watched and heard them. I am aware that given a modicum of help the wildlife of this beautiful county can thrive and renew itself each year. I also know that when the winter comes again it will bring icy blizzards to cover the cottage and garden in a mantle of deep snow and I will look out on it in the company of my beloved cats and appreciate, as always, the sheer wonders of nature. But as I look out once more, in my heart I will be remembering a particular trail of paw tracks long ago belonging to a certain cat called Toby Jug, to whom my mind can never really say goodbye. Under the snow and ice the garden itself will be resting to recoup its strength for a new beginning of growth and floral abundance. Snow-covered Owl Cottage will also be resting, sheltering and preserving the life within it and everywhere around will be in a blessed natural state of grace before awakening once more to the hustle and bustle of the active life of flora and fauna.

When the winter goes and eventually summertime comes around again, Catherine and I will sit out in the garden with our cats Luis and Max and luxuriate in the sweetness of the air and the sound of vibrant birdsong. We will talk again of early times at Owl Cottage and pay homage to the many gifts it has bestowed upon us. Owl Cottage will remain forever as a celestially favoured site where elegance and grace are waiting in readiness to stimulate the creative mind to higher things and a profound love of nature.